JUJITSU
FIGURE-4 LOCKS
Submission Holds of the Gentle Art

George Kirby

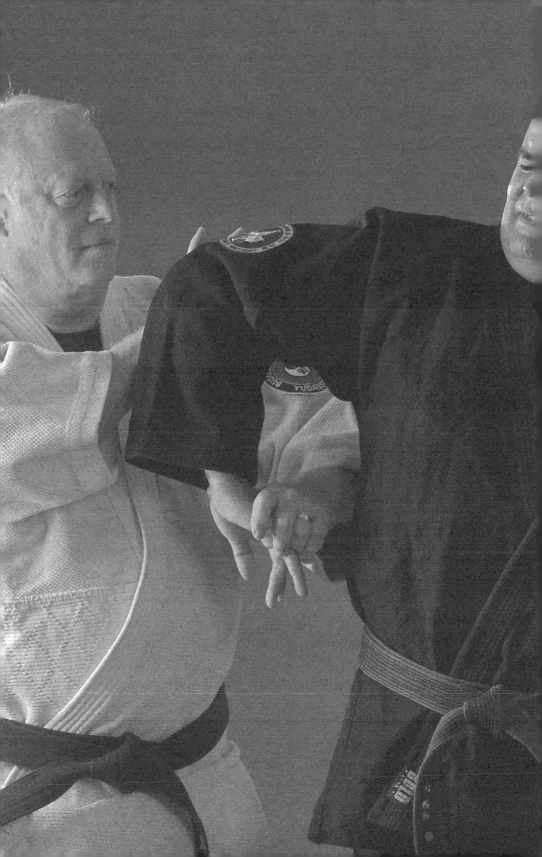

BLACK BELT B·O·O·K·S

JUJITSU FIGURE-4 LOCKS

Submission Holds of the Gentle Art

George Kirby

Edited by Sarah Dzida, Raymond Horwitz,
Jeannine Santiago and Jon Sattler

Cover and Graphic Design by John Bodine

Photography by Rick Hustead

Demonstration Partners: Mark Jordan, Marc Tucker and Steven Castorena

Library of Congress Control Number: 2009909073
ISBN-10: 0-89750-180-2
ISBN-13: 978-0-89750-180-4

First Printing 2009

WARNING

BLACK BELT BOOKS
A Division of **OHARA ▥ PUBLICATIONS, INC.**
World Leader in Martial Arts Publications

ACKNOWLEDGMENTS

After teaching *jujitsu* for almost 42 years, where do I begin? Do I begin with the faith that *sensei* Jack Sanzo Seki had in me when I took over the instructional program at the Burbank YMCA in 1968? How about professor Harold Brosious, who also took me under his wing to learn elements of *ketsugo jujitsu* even though he knew from the outset that I was trying to integrate his approach into what Seki had taught me?

Do I reflect on my first meeting with professor Wally Jay? At a tournament I was judging, Jay came over and sternly asked why I gave the contestant a zero. After my explanation, he said, "Good. You were the only one who scored him right."

Was it meeting top *jujitsuka*, such as professors Sig Kufferath, Willy Cahill, Bernie Lau and Tora Tanaka? And having the opportunity to work and learn from them at various martial arts camps and seminars?

Was it the irreplaceable opportunity of watching my students grow, not only as martial artists but also as worthwhile contributors to their own communities? Was it Adel, my wife, who always supported my goals even though it took away from "family" time?

Was it Richard Miles, the principal at Olive Vista Junior High School who encouraged me to go through the bureaucratic hoops so I could teach jujitsu as a regular class at the junior-high level? Was it the staff at Ohara/Black Belt Communications who have continued to have faith in me over the years? Or was it the opportunity to become a founding member of the Los Angeles Police Department's Civilian Martial Arts Advisory Board and serve as a defensive-tactics consultant over the years?

After almost 42 years, which really isn't a long time, the list is almost endless, and that's what makes it priceless. As I've always told my students, "Luck is when skill meets opportunity." I have been truly fortunate and truly lucky.

However, I do want to be specific in acknowledging particular individuals who helped make this book possible. First, I want to acknowledge professor Steve Heremaia, who made me aware of the concept approach to teaching a martial art. It took me almost 40 years to figure out what he meant and that it was a valid concept. I need to thank the students at my *dojo* who had to put up with my machinations while I learned how to put what I believed was Heremaia's concept approach into practice. I was pleasantly surprised that my students really benefited so much from it.

I also want to thank my demonstration partners who also provided important technical guidance when I needed it:

- Mark Jordan, a sixth-degree black belt in *budoshin* jujitsu, is one of my senior instructors. Having started his martial arts training in the military, he is currently on the national American Ju-Jitsu Association board of directors and serves as the AJA vice president and chairman of the AJA National Standards and Certification Board. He is also co-director of Camp Budoshin, a national training camp with top instructors, which is in its 17th year.

- Marc Tucker, a fifth-degree black belt in budoshin jujitsu, is my co-instructor for the Santa Clarita Budoshin Jujitsu Dojo. He is active in the AJA, serving on the national board of directors and as its treasurer.

- Steven Castorena is a fourth-degree black belt in budoshin jujitsu. He and I go back almost four decades when he was a student in my fledgling Jujitsu Club at Olive Vista Junior High in Sylmar, California.

I want to thank you three for your time and patience while serving as my attackers and advisers. Your combined technical background is hard to beat and a real asset to budoshin jujitsu and the martial arts community in general. Without you, this book would not be as thorough as it is. Even though you are my top *yudansha*, I hope that you will continue in the art and be a positive inspiration to others.

Thanks also to Sarah Dzida, who was very patient with me as I learned new book-writing skills. The "pix storyboard" turned out to be a real time-saver. Yes, an old horse can learn new tricks. Thanks also to the rest of the Black Belt staff for putting this book together and including well-placed artwork and a great cover.

ABOUT THE AUTHOR

Professor George Kirby, a 10th-degree black belt, age 65, is an internationally recognized martial arts instructor and author. He has been teaching *jujitsu* through local community agencies since 1967. He was awarded the title of *hanshi* in 1997 and his 10th-degree grade in 2000. He has taught seminars throughout the United States, Canada, Europe and Israel.

Using his skills as a martial artist and high-school teacher, Kirby has starred in an eight-DVD series and written a number of books and magazine articles. His published books include *Jujitsu: Basic Techniques of the Gentle Art* (Ohara Publications 1983), *Jujitsu: Intermediate Techniques of the Gentle Art* (Ohara Publications 1985), *Jutte: Japanese Power of Ten Hands Weapon* (Ohara Publications 1987), *Budoshin Jujitsu: "The Big Book"* 6th edition (self-published 2002), *Jujitsu Nerve Techniques: The Invisible Weapon of Self-Defense* (Ohara Publications 2001) and *Advanced Jujitsu: The Science Behind the Gentle Art* (Black Belt Communications LLC 2006). In 1992, Panther Productions released the eight-DVD video instructional series *Black Belt Ju-Jitsu*. Kirby has also written numerous articles for *Black Belt*, *Inside Karate* and other martial arts magazines.

In addition to his instructional responsibilities, Kirby serves as chairman for the board of directors for Budoshin Jujitsu Dojo Inc. (a nonprofit, educational foundation) and the American Jujitsu Association (an amateur athletic association and governing body for jujitsu and jujitsu amateur competition in the United States). He is also the founder of the Budoshin Jujitsu Yudanshakai, an educational foundation. Kirby is active in a number of other martial arts organizations, as well.

Kirby was a public-school teacher for 39 years, from 1967 until his "retirement" in 2006. He has a Master of Arts in social science/political science. He was the chairman of the social science department at U.S. Grant High School in Van Nuys, California, from 1992 to 2006.

While Kirby may have retired from teaching for the Los Angeles Unified School District, he strongly believes that retirement is relative and thus has not retired from teaching. So, in the fall of 2007, Kirby began teaching *budoshin jujitsu* at the College of the Canyons in Santa Clarita, California. He also continues to conduct seminars nationwide, teach classes through the Santa Clarita Parks and Recreation Department, organize and run the annual Budoshin Jujitsu Summer Camp (August of each year) and organize Camp Budoshin (October of each year), which is known as the "supermarket" of martial arts camps in California.

INTRODUCTION

"You can't remember everything I teach, and it's not written down anywhere. If you plan on becoming a respected *sensei*, you must be able to teach everything you have been taught."

-Jack Sanzo Seki, *jujitsu sensei*

We are born. We go through childhood and become adults. As adults, we become productive members of our community, either by having and raising children responsibly and/or through our occupation. We then retire and/or become grandparents (perhaps to get even with our children). At some point, some of us are sought out for wisdom and learning based on our experiences in life. Ultimately, we pass on to the great *tatami* up in the sky. So it is with life. We complete our life cycle and go on.

So it is with the five-step learning process I first mentioned in my second book, *Jujitsu: Intermediate Techniques of the Gentle Art* in 1985. The five steps are:

1. **Patience**—the willingness to take many small steps up the mountain at the correct pace and in a particular sequence.

2. **Repetition**—the process of embedding information in your mind so that it can be recalled instantly, seamlessly and without hesitation.

3. **Understanding**—the ability to know how and why things are as they are or why they work as they do.

4. **Experimentation**—your desire to use your acquired knowledge to find different and perhaps better ways to do things you have already learned.

5. **Evaluation**—your ability to honestly and objectively look at your growth and acquisition of knowledge and decide its validity.

The five-step learning process is universal and can be applied to many aspects of your life experience, including the martial arts. As applied to the martial arts, the first step is learning the basic movements of your art. The second is combining and repeating those movements until they become automatic and ingrained, like in *kata* practice. The third step is when you progress toward learning why certain movements occur as they do. This is a critical element in your learning process because, without it, you can't really gain any physical, theoretical or philosophical insight into your art. The fourth step in your growth as a martial artist is experimentation.

You'll start putting your technical knowledge together in different ways. Some of your combinations and ideas will work, and some won't. That's part of this stage of the learning process. The fifth step, self-evaluation, is the most critical. It's at this point that you recognize what and how much you've learned, what your proficiency is and what your next step is—that is if you're sincere in your growth of a particular martial art.

In essence, you've come full circle—almost. Your growth has been like that of a five-ringed spiral graph.

Single Spiral Graph

Each oval in the spiral graph represents one of the steps in the five-step process.

However, you will never really return to the start of that particular process. If you are serious about growth, you will go through a series of five-step sequences. If you are truly serious about growth in your martial art, this will become a lifelong endeavor.

Multiple Spiral Graph

Most people will go through sequences of the five-step learning process numerous times throughout their lives. The completion of one five-step process leads to the start of another. As this drawing illustrates, this becomes your life sequence.

As a schoolteacher, parent and martial arts instructor, I have always believed in the five-step learning process and life sequence. I believe in it because it always returns you to the beginning—or to your roots, so to speak. However, as you move from step five (evaluation), to step one (patience), you do it with a realization that your roots or base have changed. Because of gained knowledge, insight or wisdom from the learning process, you can't go back to "square one."

You can't go back to square one for two reasons. First, it's no longer there. Second, and more important, you can't go back to step one because you can't "wipe your slate clean" because prior experiences will affect how you think and act, even if you try to disregard them.

Just as a side note, the place between step five and step one is where patience comes from. From serious self-evaluation, you come to understand the virtue and value of patience. You can either rush in ruthless pursuit after something, never really acquiring it, or you can develop the skills that will help it come to you.

Going back to square one would also be counterproductive. You would have to clean your slate. You would also have to clean everyone else's slate. It would become necessary to recreate the original environment, and you would then be destined to repeat the process and learning you had gone through. It would be like moving in a circle and going nowhere. It is much more productive to grow from your experiences and hopefully become a better person and a greater contributor to society.

So what does this very short philosophical discourse have to do with growth in the martial arts and this book in particular? Everything.

If you are a martial artist, you are going through sequences of multiple five-step learning processes. At the most basic, the first step was when you started as an inept and ignorant neophyte in whatever martial art you began in. In step two, you constantly reviewed the skills you acquired in an attempt to master and truly understand your art. If you wanted to help assure your success in this area, you took notes on what you were learning for later reflection and practice. As you moved on to the third step, you may have had the skill and opportunity to teach the art to others. At the fourth step, you may have been fortunate enough to become teachers of teachers and thus perpetuate your art. Some of you may even have become fortunate enough to reach the fifth level—to publish your knowledge either in print or video, thus establishing and standardizing your art beyond your lifetime. Your journey through the martial arts is another manifestation of the five-step learning process, except that it's been repeated many times over to become a life sequence.

However, in my life sequence, something happened during the five-step process that became the rationale for this book. I went through a five-step learning process that altered my thinking about the art over the past four decades. The first step (patience) began back in the 1960s and early 1970s when I was in professors Jack Sanzo Seki and Harold Brosious' *jujitsu* classes. Seki would say to us students, "You can't remember everything I teach, and it's not written down anywhere. If you plan on becoming a respected *sensei*, you must be able to teach everything you have been taught." Because I took Seki's words seriously, I made a personal commitment to compile my own notes on all the techniques Seki taught. I was among the few of his students who took notes (before and after we became black belts), even though Seki also chided us about taking them. Seki's chiding was part of the psychological harassment that he shelled out periodically and without remorse on the mat. However, those few of us who took notes were the ones who became successful teachers of jujitsu.

After several years of note-taking and repeatedly practicing the techniques that Seki taught, we "note-takers" realized how much information we had because of all the notes we had taken. I also realized that I was in the depths of the second step of the five-step process (repetition). I ultimately compiled more than 850 techniques and variations from Seki and Brosious. I had ample time to practice the techniques over and over again, correcting my notes as I improved my understanding of the characteristics of each technique. I regularly and patiently typed all my technique notes onto 3-by-5-inch index cards in the late 1970s before the computer age. (Eventually, I would compile them all into my core teaching manual, *Budoshin Jujitsu: The Big Book*, which I first published in the early 1980s. It is still used by most of my black belts.) By repeatedly practicing the techniques, I reinforced my "muscle memory" of them. By writing and rewriting my observations of the body movements of each technique, I also reinforced my ability to effectively and clearly explain how each jujitsu technique was properly executed.

Eight hundred fifty is a big number. However, there are a couple of realities to balance out this huge amount of information. First, I realized early on that I couldn't remember all 850-plus techniques at the same time. Second, I realized that there were only 20 to 30 of all those techniques that were part of my personal repertoire at one time. Fortunately, even if asked today, I was wise enough to say that I didn't know them all. I was not about to insert my foot in my mouth.

In the 1980s, I moved on to step three of the learning process (understanding). I had the opportunity to meet professor Steve Heremaia, a well-respected jujitsu instructor at Camp Danzan Ryu, near Monterey, California. He had reduced the study of jujitsu down to 10 "concept" techniques that formed the basis of his system. For many years after I met him, I had great difficulty in understanding or accepting his approach to teaching the art. I had so many techniques collected from my own studies that I couldn't see the simplicity of his approach. I couldn't see the forest because of all the trees. It took me 25 years of writing jujitsu books to recognize the validity of his approach.

Heremaia's approach toward teaching jujitsu served as a springboard for writing my previous book, *Advanced Jujitsu: The Science Behind the Gentle Art*. His approach eventually helped me recognize the relationship and similarities among many diverse techniques. The process of achieving this recognition was the result of experimentation (step four in the learning process) with the many movements in jujitsu to find commonalities or similar movements that resulted in similar or identical responses. However, before I could move forward in this direction, I realized that there was a missing foundation that I had to establish before I could further explore what I believed was Heremaia's teaching approach to jujitsu.

Writing *Advanced Jujitsu* was another five-step process, in addition to the one that started 40 years ago. The book helped me break down my 850-plus jujitsu techniques into a more usable collection of basic movements that students could learn and use more effectively.

With the knowledge and insight gained from writing *Advanced Jujitsu*, I started to see close and definitive common elements among different techniques that I had previously not realized. It was at this point that I had moved to step five (evaluation). I started seeing common movements among divergent techniques. Was this what Heremaia was referring to by his "concept" techniques? I still don't have all the answers to that question, but that doesn't worry me because learning is part of the life sequence.

Once *Advanced Jujitsu* was completed, it had a tremendous and unintended impact on how I looked at the art and how I would teach the art from that point onward. By using the concepts presented in *Advanced Jujitsu*, I have radically changed how I teach many basic techniques. As a result, students are learning jujitsu techniques more effectively and more quickly. Advanced students see the logic to what they have learned and how physics and kinesthetics apply to the art. This was not part of the "plan," but it happened almost intuitively. Writing that book served as a turning point for my beginning to understand my art in its virtual simplicity.

My first two books dealt with learning specific skills to reach specific goals (belt ranks). My third book, *Jujitsu Nerve Techniques*, dealt with another specific skill. My most recent book, *Advanced Jujitsu*, was a transitional book. It was my first book that really dealt with teaching concepts based on a scientific process. It also had the unintended result of getting me to think of the art of jujitsu differently. So *Jujitsu Figure-4 Locks* is my first concept book, which tries to simplify learning the art. What's the difference between specific skills and concepts? Growth is an inevitable never-ending process if you keep an open mind. Continue with me as I climb the mountain. The poem below, which first appeared in *Jujitsu: Intermediate Techniques of the Gentle Art*, adds another verse in this book to act as a guide as you move up the mountainside. I sincerely hope that this book will serve as a learning tool for you as much as it will for me. Who knows what you'll learn and discover as you continue upward and who knows what surprise will meet you when you reach the peak.

As a lifelong student of jujitsu, you have the responsibility to pass on everything you've been taught, especially if you have the opportunity to teach the art to others. That's why studying any martial art is more than just a five-step learning process; it is a life sequence.

Two Inseparable Friends

Control is the key.	Control is the ki.
Patience is the key.	Patience is the ki.
The key is not trying at all.	The ki is not trying at all.
Self-control is the key.	Self-control is the ki.
Ki is the key to success	Ki is the ki to success.
Simplicity is the key.	Simplicity is the ki.
Humbleness is the key.	Humbleness is the ki.
Inner calm is the key.	Inner calm is the ki.
Mushin* is the key.	Mushin is the ki.
Ki is the key to success.	Ki is the ki to success.
The concept is the key.	The concept is the ki.
Understanding is the key.	Understanding is the ki.
Mushin allows you to apply the key.	Mushin allows you to apply the ki.
Your ki will be the key.	Your ki will be the ki.
Ki is the key to success.	Ki is the ki to success.

*Footnote: *Mushin* is Japanese for "no mind." For a more complete definition, refer to the glossary at the end of this book.

TABLE OF CONTENTS

Acknowledgments...4

About the Author..6

Introduction...8

PART ONE

Chapter 1: Setting the Foundation.............................17

    Axes 18

    Joint-Chain Hierarchy..20

    Leverage 21

    Axial Rotation and Torque 24

Chapter 2: Building the Framework............................32

    Common Attributes..32

    Consistent Control Movements 40

    Standard Steps 42

    Locking a Joint-Chain Hierarchy 47

Chapter 3: Finishing the House—The Small Stuff Is Important...51

    Ki Flow..51

    Hand Grip vs. Hook for Effective Leverage 56

    Pronation vs. Supination..61

    Foot and Torso Placement..72

    Keep Hold of the Extremity: Resistance Is Futile 85

Chapter 4: The Street and the Dojo—A Sense of Direction.........92

PART TWO
Chapter 5: Figure-4 Locks...95
  A Serious Word of Caution! 95
  Armbars and Arm Locks 98
  Shoulder Locks 114
  Leg and Hip Locks 144
  Pins and Chokes 158
  Miscellaneous Techniques 169

Concluding Remarks..178
Glossary for *Figure-4 Locks*..180

PART ONE

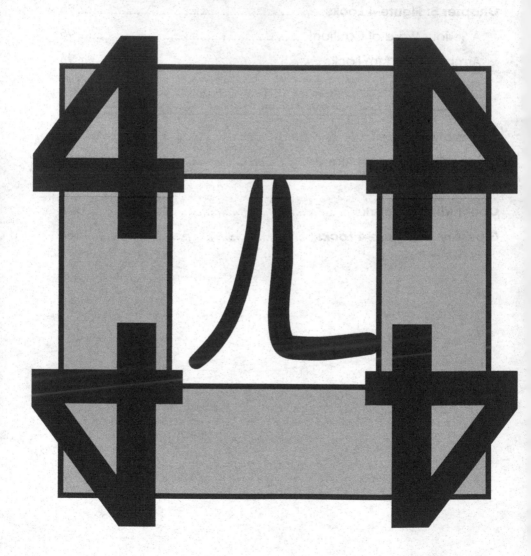

CHAPTER 1
Setting the Foundation

For me, writing has always been about discovery, mainly in terms of theory because there has to be a background or valid explanation as to why a martial art and its techniques, like *jujitsu* and figure-4 locks, work. The execution of the techniques becomes more viable by discovering, accepting and understanding those backgrounds and explanations.

For the most part, many well-trained jujitsu instructors have developed this depth of knowledge. They also have a sincere desire to convey it to their students. However, all this knowledge can be a liability and an asset in the teaching process. It's a liability because jujitsu instructors have a tendency to get caught up in detailed explanations of the theory behind the application of the technique. As a result, students need to relearn the technique even after the lengthy explanation because they've forgotten what to do. This is the unfortunate outcome of long explanations.

However, all this information is an asset to jujitsu instructors because it means they have the knowledge necessary to teach the physical and technical aspects of techniques. The instructors understand the theory behind what makes them work, and students should (and do) ask questions, which they have the right to have answered in a way they understand. This not only helps them learn the art more effectively in the long run but also provides them with a strong technical and theoretical base when they become teachers themselves. In fact, part of my goal in writing this book is to help you develop the technical and theoretical base to execute figure-4 locks correctly and to be able to rationally and competently explain what you're doing to someone else—or maybe your own students some day.

The reason most "traditional" jujitsu books have a lot of theory in them is because the authors have learned through their life sequences that theory is essential to the successful execution of techniques and learning the art. This book will not be any different. I will probably increase my understanding of the art simply by writing this book. In the process, I hope to help you develop a sound background in the concepts behind figure-4 locks. Specifically, I want to demonstrate how and why they work, the common elements and movements inherent in all figure-4 locks, and how to apply these concepts in an orderly and effective manner. This will allow you to use any figure-4 lock more effectively.

You might be asking, Why select figure-4 locks for my first concept book (or book dealing with a specific concept of jujitsu)? It's a legitimate question. My response is that figure-4 locks are used to set up a tremendous number of jujitsu throws as well as 90 percent to 95 percent of the pins, locks, holds and submissions used in the art. The concepts involved in effective figure-4 locks are found in almost every locking technique in jujitsu. The effective and efficient use of these concepts behind figure-4 locks will have a snowball effect on almost everything you do in jujitsu. Once you start applying your newly acquired knowledge, it will be like replacing a flashlight with a floodlight. And yes, the realization of these concepts and how they work has had a tremendous impact on how I now teach the art of jujitsu, even after 42 years of studying it. Now the art is so much simpler.

However, before I begin, I need to reintroduce some of the basic technical information from my last book, *Advanced Jujitsu: The Science Behind the Gentle Art*. A lot of the technical information for *Jujitsu Figure-4 Locks* will be based on *Advanced Jujitsu* for the reasons I gave in the introduction to this book. These four things are:

1) axes (x, y, and z),
2) joint hierarchy,
3) leverage, and
4) axial rotation and torque.

Axes

Knowing the role of an axis is important to the success of every martial art and sport. Axes determine how a body will move and how to move it most effectively. Every person has three axes. The x-axis is a line that goes through the center point (*saiki tanden*) of your body (about two inches below the navel) and extends outward to the left and right of your center point, parallel to your hips and torso. Your y-axis is a line perpendicular to the ground that extends up through the vertical centerline of your body and through your center point. Your z-axis is another line that is parallel to the surface, extending forward and backward through your body at your center point. If you remember basic geometry and x-y-z graphs, you'll also realize that your center point is point (0, 0, 0) on the graph. Knowledge of axes can help you understand the centerline of your body and extremities. It can help you establish an attacker's center of balance as well as learn how to disturb it (*kuzushi*). If you can move your attacker so that his y-axis is not perpendicular to the ground, which means that his x-axis and z-axis are not parallel to the ground, then your attacker will be off-balanced. Off-balancing can be done in a variety of ways, including:

- pulling or pushing your attacker in one direction or another, which forces him to step in one direction or another in an attempt to regain his balance;

- a hit or kick that will force him to bend in one direction or another or lose his footing in one direction or another; and

- an action initiated by your attacker in which he tries to grab or hit you and must take a step forward or move his body forward, whether or not you move out of the way.

All these actions move the attacker's center point from (0, 0, 0) on his x, y and z axes to some place else, and that is what can off-balance him. It can help you determine an assailant's angle of attack and how best to deal with it as the following pictures will illustrate.

X-Y-Z Axes

This picture shows the x, y and z axes of the defender (right) and the attacker. By recognizing these axes, you can visualize that the attacker is off-balance because he has moved off his vertical y-axis as he has reached forward with his right hand and grabbed the lapel of the defender's uniform.

By recognizing in what direction your attacker is off-balancing himself, you can determine what movements you will make to further off-balance your attacker and which figure-4 lock(s) can be used more effectively to establish control over him. For example, if your attacker swings at you, you can deflect his hit outward. If you move out of the direction of his hit, this will cause his hit to go farther than anticipated, thus off-balancing him more. If he grabs you with one hand, you can sidestep or pivot to your right, left, or even take a step back to further off-balance him. In jujitsu, this is called "helping" your attacker go in the direction he wants to go. Once the attacker is off-balanced, then you can go into a figure-4 lock suitable to his off-balanced position.

Every joint also has a center point and x, y and z axes. This is important to figure-4 locks because if you rotate a joint off its center point, it creates a chain reaction that will also move the body's center point off its axes. Rotating a joint off its axes is also the movement you use to set a lock.

Joint-Chain Hierarchy

Take a moment to really look at yourself. You have numerous joints in your body that can be generally categorized into three types: fibrous (which don't move), cartilaginous (which have limited movement) and synovial (which move freely within their structure). The joints I am referring to in *Jujitsu Figure-4 Locks* are synovial joints, all the way from the last joint, in your little finger to your shoulder joint or from your toes to your hip joint, respectively. Each extremity has a joint-chain hierarchy or order. The joint that connects to your torso (shoulders and hips) is called a parent joint. All other joints beyond the parent joints are referred to as child joints. Your attacker also has the same joint-chain hierarchy.

The ultimate goal of locking any child joint is to control and lock a parent joint. Locking a parent joint will move the center point of the attacker. This, in turn, will off-balance the attacker and make the figure-4 lock or any throw or takedown related to it relatively easy to execute.

Controlling Child Joints

This picture shows how controlling a child joint, pushing down on the attacker's right elbow, can cause the parent joint (attacker's shoulder) to move forward, thus off-balancing the attacker's body.

Leverage

Leverage is the mechanical advantage achieved through the use of a lever to move an object. Effective leverage thereby allows a smaller person to throw a larger person or, in the case of figure-4 locks, allows you to lock the joint hierarchy of an extremity, thus locking the parent joint of the extremity and consequently unbalancing your attacker's body with relatively little effort.

In order to effectively execute all figure-4 locks and many judo throws, you need to have an understanding of how first-class levers are set up and work. This is because all figure-4 locks and many judo throws depend on well-set first-class levers. In a first-class lever, the fulcrum (pivot point of the lever) is between the effort (amount of energy or force required) and load (mass of the item moved by the lever).

Effort	Fulcrum	Load
E	F	L

$$\Delta$$

First-class levers are the simplest levers because the fulcrum is between the effort and load. Your goal is to use minimum effort in executing any jujitsu technique that helps you know that you're doing it properly.

The three pictures below provide simple examples of first-class levers used in the process of setting up figure-4 locks. In each case, the hold is properly set. Note that in each example, the attacker's child and parent joints are locked, he is off his y-axis as his back is arched and he is off-balanced. Injury is inevitable in all three scenarios if any additional effort is applied by the defender.

First-Class Levers

Shoulder Lock

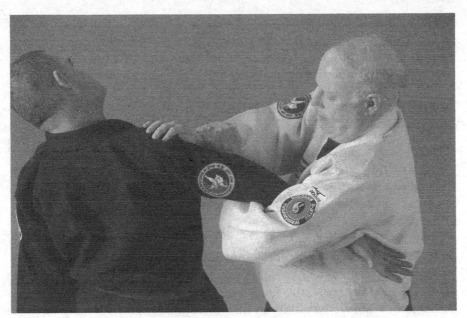

Armbar

Hip Lock

By practicing and understanding how levers work, you will have a better grasp of why your figure-4 locks work as they do. The leverage achieved through the use of levers in figure-4 locks will alter the balance of your attacker's body, thus giving you a mechanical advantage over your attacker.

Axial Rotation and Torque

Axial rotation occurs when you turn or twist a part of the body like a child joint (arm, leg, head, finger, toe, hand, foot) along its length or y-axis. Turning any extremity on its y-axis will eventually cause all the joints above that joint, including the parent, to rotate and lock. Sufficient axial rotation will off-balance the attacker and possibly cause joint injuries in the process.

Synovial joints don't just suddenly stop moving. As you turn a joint off its center point (such as the joints of the wrist, elbow or shoulder, or a foot, knee or hip), the ligaments and tendons will stretch to a certain degree. Once they reach the limitation of their stretching ability, the synovial joint will lose its ability to turn or rotate on its y-axis any farther. The shapes of the bones in the joint are also a factor in how far a joint will turn. You will notice increasing resistance to the turn as you attempt to farther rotate an opponent's joint. This increasing resistance is known as joint dampening. Once you dampen a joint to its maximum, it will not rotate any farther, regardless of how much torque you apply, unless you plan to injure that joint.

Torque is the amount of effort, energy or force applied to the twisting motion around the y-axis. Excessive torquing, which can extend the joint beyond its joint-dampening capabilities, is what will cause joint injuries to occur. Injuries can occur to the initial child joint that was locked as well as the other joints in the joint hierarchy. Excessive torquing can also result in "green-branch" or stress fractures to the straight bones along the y-axis of the torqued extremity.

At this point, you may be asking; "If all this twisting and rotating is causing joint dampening and not locking, then why are figure-4 locks not called figure-4 joint dampening?" Generally, the word "lock" means that if you set a hold on a joint and the joint cannot be moved any farther, the joint is locked. Lock is not really the right word to use. A "lock" really only occurs when everything is stuck in one position without any external force being applied to maintain the position. If a nail is held in a vice, it is locked there. If your car door closes and doesn't open without you pushing the door latch or button, it is locked in place. The word lock has probably been historically used because it is a simpler term that conveys the idea of what is physically happening to a particular joint hierarchy when it is sufficiently torqued through axial rotation to the point at which resistance and joint dampening would occur. The joint has, in essence, been locked, although your external effort is required to maintain it.

⸻ ⌒⌒ ⸻

It is very important to understand the role and actions of axial rotation and torquing, as well as axes, leverage and joint-chain hierarchy. When you put all this together, you will recognize how they can affect body movement. You will discover how, when and why all figure-4 locks and actions on the human body work as they do. You will also recognize how figure-4 locks act as a key to putting the above elements into play in a coherent manner.

The basic hand throw serves as an excellent visual example of the application of a figure-4 lock resulting in an effective throw using the axes, axial rotation, joint hierarchy, leverage and torque on the attacker. If you bend the attacker's right hand in toward his forearm and turn it outward slightly along the y-axis of the attacker's arm with axial rotation, it is possible to use a first-class lever (as described earlier) to torque and lock the wrist—a child joint. If you continue to apply pressure to the back of the attacker's hand, the continuous torque on the attacker's wrist will lock his elbow joint. The attacker's elbow will then turn inward toward his body. This action will, in turn, lock the attacker's shoulder or parent joint, thus forcing his body to lean back to compensate for the torque applied to his shoulder. The attacker is now off-balance. All three of his axes have been moved out of alignment from their natural positions. You continue to apply the leverage toward the attacker's elbow, thus torquing the attacker's shoulder and off-balancing the attacker more. You then rotate your body counterclockwise (to your left) on your y-axis to guide the attacker's fall so he lands at your feet.

Basic Hand Throw (*Te Nage*) With Axes and Rotation

The attacker (in the black *gi*) grabs the defender's lapel. The defender is in a balanced position, whereas the attacker is not. The attacker's own movement off-balances his own center point.

The defender hooks on the attacker's right wrist with his left hand.

The defender turns to his right (clockwise) to off-balance the attacker. He also pushes down at the attacker's forearm, just below his elbow to bend his arm and bring his body forward, thus altering the y-axis of the attacker and unbalancing him.

He turns back to his left (counter-clockwise), holding the hand of the attacker against his chest. This movement initiates the figure-4 lock on the attacker's wrist.

Note: Your right palm rests on top of the your left thumb, which is pressing down on a pressure point on the back of the attacker's hand. This initiates the first class lever at the attacker's wrist and sets up a figure-4 lock.

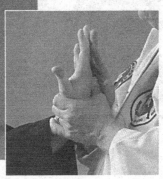

Continued ➤

The defender steps in with his right foot at the same time so that he will be in a balanced position when he executes the hand throw.

Note: The defender's y-axis will be reasonably close to the attacker's y-axis, thus replacing it as the hand throw is executed.

With his arms in and close to his sides, the defender keeps the hand of the attacker against his chest as much as possible.

Note: The defender pushes the attacker's hand toward his y-axis of the arm at the elbow—not turning the wrist to left. This pushing motion may make it difficult or impossible to keep his hand against the defender's chest.

This sets the figure-4 lock of the attacker's wrist and allows the torque from this lock to transfer to the attacker's right shoulder joint through joint hierarchy and axial rotation.

The defender continues to push the attacker's bent hand toward the y-axis of the attacker's arm in a line that would go just past the outside of his right elbow to off-balance him.

Note: Do NOT turn his wrist to the left. This will eventually lock all the joints in the arm because of joint hierarchy and axial rotation, thus applying a figure-4 lock to his shoulder.

Once the hand throw is properly set up, the defender can pivot his left foot back counterclockwise to rotate on his y-axis while keeping his elbows as close to his sides as possible.

Continued

The lock allows the defender to execute the throw.

The throw brings the attacker down to the ground. From this point, a number of different figure-4 lock submissions can be applied to the attacker.

You will understand this part of the scientific explanation because it's simple, consistent and universal to all techniques dealing with joint locks. This "physical awareness" is essential to effectively execute figure-4 locks and control your attacker. If you develop a physical awareness of how an attacker's body reacts to your execution of figure-4 locks, you will know when they are working properly because your attacker is moving where you want him to and how you want him to. This physical awareness will also allow you to apply more or less effort as necessary to execute the figure-4 lock successfully. By physically sensing your attacker's reaction to your figure-4 lock, you will also have a good awareness of how much pain or discomfort you are causing. This ultimately allows you to control your attacker more effectively, depending on the situation you are in.

Chapter 2
Building the Framework

In Chapter 1, I presented the four elements that will help you establish a firm foundation for figure-4 locks. These are the technical elements that sound figure-4 locks are built on. However, successful figure-4 locks also require a solid framework on which the rest of the house can be completed, and this is what you will learn in this chapter.

To build a strong figure-4 framework, you need the following aspects:

- common attributes
- consistent control movements
- basic setup
- locking a joint-chain hierarchy

Common Attributes

All figure-4 locks have a common set of attributes. First, you should be able to see the No. "4" in any figure-4 lock that you set up, regardless of which of your and your attacker's joints are bent or straight.

Standing Figure-4 Armbar With Figure-4 Superimposed on the Armbar

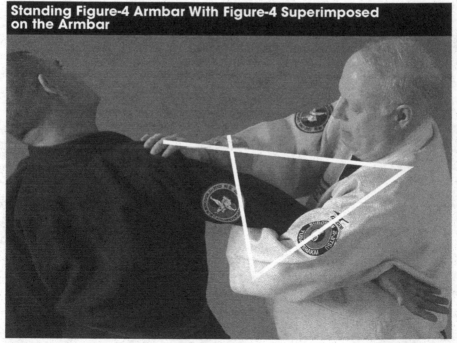

Note how the No. "4" is visible in this figure-4 lock.

You should be able to visualize the No. "4" in the following figure-4 locks. Your ability to visually perceive the No. "4" in your lock will quickly tell you whether you have a viable lock on your attacker.

Basic Shoulder-Lock Comealong

In this variation of the basic shoulder lock, the defender has set up a rear shoulder-lock comealong after he has countered a handshake by the attacker intended to trap the defender's right hand.

Basic Figure-4 Arm Lock

In this setup of an arm lock, the defender's left forearm is under the attacker's forearm, and the defender's left hand is hooked on the attacker's right shoulder or upper arm.

Knife-Edge Arm Lock

In this setup of an arm lock, the defender's left forearm is under the attacker's forearm, and the defender's left hand is formed into a knife-edge in the attacker's right shoulder joint.

Figure-4 Leg Lock

This is a well-set figure-4 leg lock. When the defender sets this lock, he makes sure that the attacker's foot is pointed to the defender's outside. If it's pointed to the inside (toward his y-axis), he will have enough leverage to break the lock.

Second, the situation will determine how you will set up your figure-4.

In the picture below, a shoulder lock has been set. In this figure-4 lock, a second type of the No. "4" can be seen. Compare it to the figure-4 lock on page 32. In that standing figure-4 armbar, the defender's elbow is bent at 90 degrees or less (more acute) while the attacker's arm is straight (180 degrees). In the figure-4 shoulder lock below, the attacker's elbow is bent at an angle of 90 degrees or less instead of in a straight line. You will also note that the defender's right hand has also bent the attacker's right hand at his wrist, thus setting a wrist press almost identical to the basic hand throw. When sufficient upward pressure is quickly applied to the back of the attacker's elbow by the defender's forearm, the attacker's elbow will probably dislocate, so please use caution when practicing this lock.

Figure-4 Shoulder Lock

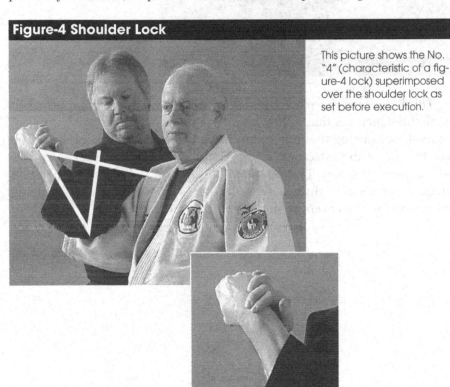

This picture shows the No. "4" (characteristic of a figure-4 lock) superimposed over the shoulder lock as set before execution.

This insert shows how an additional figure-4 lock has been placed on the attacker's wrist as described above in the text.

Figure-4 Shoulder-Lock Variation

This is an alternate shot of a figure-4 shoulder lock.

Note: The attacker's wrist is NOT bent in this variation.

Third, once you have a figure-4 set, you have control of your attacker. In all three pictures that follow, control is established through the use of figure-4 locks using the joint-chain hierarchy and first-class levers. The parent joint of the extremity is locked, thus forcing the attacker into an off-balanced position. The defender can control the attacker's position through the use of slightly increased effort to a child joint, thus applying more stress to the parent joint of the extremity.

Shoulder-Lock Rear Comealong

In this simplified co-mealong, the attacker's right wrist is braced against the inside of the defender's upper arm. If the defender uses his left hand to pull the attacker's right arm farther back, the defender can cause additional pain to the attacker's right wrist, a child joint. This will cause the attacker to arch farther back, thus off-balancing the attacker even more.

Figure-4 Armbar

As the defender applies upward pressure just below the attacker's elbow and slight downward pressure at the attacker's shoulder, the locked elbow, a child joint, causes the shoulder joint, a parent joint, to lock, thus off-balancing the attacker.

Little-Finger Brace

On a much smaller scale, the same concepts of the figure-4 lock, joint-chain hierarchy and leverage can be applied to smaller extremities, such as the little finger of the attacker. The defender's goal should be to use pain to secure compliance rather than to just break bones or dislocate the joints of the little finger.

Interestingly enough from an even more esoteric view, setting this type of a figure-4 lock at times will also create a square shape similar to the square outline of the Japanese No. 4: 四. (See page 39.) In this square, child joints can be hinged at either two of the opposite/diagonal corners or two corners of a single side.

Shoulder-Lock Counter

Notice the "square" shape of the shoulder-lock counter, which can be used if the attacker bends his right arm as the defender sets up a figure-4 armbar. By letting him bend his arm, the attacker will set himself up for a figure-4 shoulder lock.

Hip Lock

You can visualize the same figure-4 lock "square" in the hip lock that is being demonstrated in this picture.

Figure-4 Reverse Wrist Press

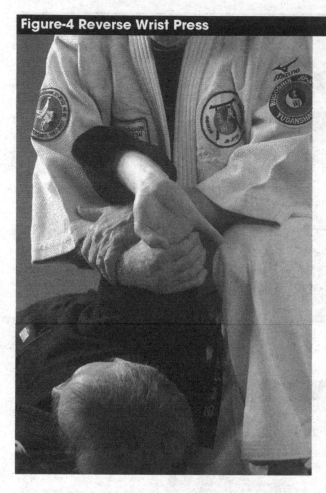

The cover shot for *Figure-4 Locks* also provides an excellent example of this esoteric view of the technique.

Consistent Control Movements

Consistent control movements are the things you do to maintain control of the attacker while remaining in a natural and balanced position during the execution of a figure-4 lock. These movements may range from making sure a joint lock is fully set before you use axial rotation and torque to moving into a balanced position (y-axis) so that the attacker is off-balance and/or rotating, so the attacker does not realize a lock has been set until it's too late to do anything about it. Consistent control movements also include proper footwork so that you can maintain your balance. This allows you to quickly and smoothly move into setting up effective figure-4 locks without the attacker becoming sufficiently aware of what you're doing. If he is unaware of your intentions or doesn't sense any effort on your part as you're setting up the figure-4 lock, he will be less likely to resist or attempt to counter what you are doing.

When doing a consistent control movement, your body is in a balanced position—it is aligned on all axes—and your extremities are naturally moving to maximize your attacker and your *ki* flow. As a result, you operate more efficiently because your ki can supplement the attacker's ki flow as necessary to control him and execute the technique you are using to subdue him. You will also have to use fewer actual steps to execute effective figure-4 locks.

By using consistent control movements, such as effective footwork, body rotation, standardized grips and holds, and extremity rotation, it is possible for you, as the defender, to set basic figure-4 locks and other holds before the attacker has realized what has happened. You will discover that you can accomplish the basic setups for figure-4 locks smoothly and easily. Execution of the figure-4 locks is then only a simple matter of continuing the direction of your motion, setting the lock, and letting the attacker use his ki to execute the technique. It can be a takedown, throw or comealong, whatever the situation demands.

Shoulder-Lock Comealong for a Handshake

The defender is in the final set position for a shoulder-lock rear comealong used against a handshake. Just as a side

Note: Sometimes an attacker will want to "shake hands" with you with the ulterior motive of trapping your right hand so you can't use it.

Standard Steps

Block it, wrap it, lock it and rotate it are the only four steps needed to secure and execute effective figure-4 locks. Follow these four basic steps, and you will always set up a figure-4 lock. The four steps are the following:

1. **Block it:** Using your forearm singly (for a hit) as a block or to deflect the attacker's hit, or doubly in a cross-block (for a kick) to deflect or block the attacker's leg. You can also use your knee to deflect or block a leg attack.

2. **Wrap it:** Wrapping one of your arms or legs around the attacking extremity as appropriate to the figure-4 lock.

3. **Lock it:** Using the other arm or your body as a brace or base to secure the figure-4 lock.

4. **Rotate it:** Moving the attacker's extremity (push, pull, rotation on the extremity's y-axis or applying pressure to the x-axis of the extremity joint) to execute the figure-4 lock.

The following sequence of pictures showing the execution of an armbar winding throw provides an example of the four-step process. Even though there are only four steps in the photo sequence that follows, additional photos are shown to present the transition from step to step.

Armbar Winding Throw
(*Ude Guruma Makikomi*)

The defender (right) and the attacker are in a ready position.

Step 1—Block it: The defender blocks the attacker's hit with his left forearm. Also, the defender steps forward with his left foot so that his and the attacker's y-axis are more closely aligned with each other.

Step 2—Wrap it: The defender starts to wrap his left arm around the attacking extremity (right arm of the attacker) in a clockwise circle. The defender needs to do the motion in a large enough circle so that ...

... the middle of his left forearm hits the attacker's right elbow from the side of his arm either at or just below his elbow. Also note that the defender's right hand is resting on the right shoulder of the attacker.

Continued ➤

Step 3—Lock it: Once contact with his elbow is made, step three of setting up a figure-4 lock begins. The defender will rotate his right arm slightly counterclockwise through moderate pressure applied with his left forearm to the outside of the attacker's right elbow.

This will result in a very secure grip of the right arm of the attacker. Also, his elbow will be facing up, which sets up the defender to execute the armbar.

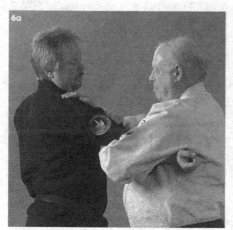

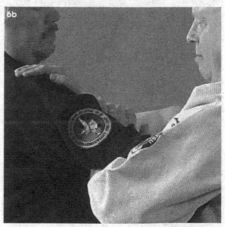

This close-up shows a proper armbar setup (figure-4 lock) at this point. The defender's left hand is also setting up a "hook" onto his right forearm.

Note: The attacker's right hand (past the defender's armpit) is palm-up, a quick indicator that the elbow of the attacker has been turned into the proper position for an armbar.

This close-up shows a proper "hook" with the defender's left hand (thumb on same side as his fingers) resting on his right forearm rather than his left hand grabbing his own right arm (thumb on underside of his arm). The advantage of the "hook" is described later in this book. The defender's right arm acts as a brace (or base) to secure the figure-4 lock.

To start the execution of the throw, the defender presses down slightly on the attacker's shoulder with his right hand while he applies a small amount of upward pressure with his left forearm.

This same effect can be accomplished by simply straightening the defender's arms slightly as he maintains the figure-4 armbar.

When the defender feels the attacker's right shoulder move up slightly (also notice his right leg is bent and his right foot is not solidly on the ground), that is an indication that the joint-chain hierarchy has been locked and he is off-balance.

Step 4—Rotate it: The defender pivots his left leg back.

Continued →

The pivot allows him to execute the throw.

Note: Out of courtesy and safety during practice, relax the figure-4 lock slightly. It can be quickly reset once the attacker is on the ground. In a street situation, you will very likely dislocate the attacker's elbow when he is thrown if you maintain a tight figure-4 lock on his arm.

If the defender goes down to the ground with the attacker, he goes down on his right knee with his left instep against the back of the attacker's head. The defender makes sure the attacker is on his right side. If he sets him up in this position—by simply maintaining the hold and thrusting his hips forward—it will be next to impossible for him to counter before the defender executes the submission.

Note: You have a variety of other figure-4 locks and other submissions that can be applied from this safe position.

Locking a Joint-Chain Hierarchy

Locking a joint-chain hierarchy is essential to an effective figure-4 lock, or to be more correct, it is an essential consequence of a correctly set figure-4 lock. After setting a figure-4 lock on a child joint—say the wrist—joint-chain hierarchy will occur when axial rotation and torque will automatically lock the next child joint and so on until the parent joint is locked.

In more technical terms, when the last child joint in a joint-chain hierarchy is "locked" (it can't be rotated any farther on its y-axis) because of a set figure-4 lock, joint dampening or resistance, axial rotation continues to be applied to the next child joint until it locks, as well. With the continuous application of torque along the y-axis, other child joints in the joint-chain hierarchy will also "lock up" until torque is applied to the parent joint. This then forces the attacker's torso off-balance and in the direction of the rotation, which is along the y-axis of the extremity.

The three pictures that follow provide examples of how using figure-4 locks secure joint-chain hierarchies, forcing the body into an off-balanced position and making it easier to execute the "throw" on your attacker.

Using the Y-Axis

In this picture, note how the attacker's arched back is set in this rear shoulder-lock comealong. The arch can be accentuated for the purpose of guiding the controlled attacker in any direction. The y-axis of the attacker's right arm is rotated in a counterclockwise direction, using joint-chain hierarchy, to accentuate and off-balance the attacker.

Locking the Shoulder Joint

In this arm-lock takedown, the attacker is being effectively controlled because his upper arm is being rotated in a clockwise direction, thus locking his shoulder joint. The attacker, therefore, is in an unbalanced forward position.

Locking the Joint-Chain Hierarchy

In this picture, locking the joint-chain hierarchy of the attacker's leg occurs by rotating the attacker's foot in a clockwise direction. It off-balances him so that he leans away from the defender. This rotating motion is the consequence of an effectively set figure-4 lock at the attacker's ankle joint.

In the case of figure-4 locks, joint-chain hierarchy causes two outcomes. Either the original child joint (first child joint that is locked in a joint-chain hierarchy) will be dislocated or the parent joint will become separated or dislocated.

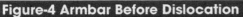

Figure-4 Armbar Before Dislocation

The elbow of the defender's arm is bent at a 90-degree angle or less, and the elbow of the attacker's arm is in a straight line (180 degrees). The picture illustrates the position of the attacker just before having his elbow dislocated. He is completely off-balance (all of his axes are out of alignment) as a result of the figure-4 armbar completely locking the joint-chain hierarchy of his right arm.

Hip Lock Before Dislocation

The attacker's knee joint is bent at a 90-degree angle or less, and the knee joint of the defender's leg is bent (usually from 135 degrees to 45 degrees). The continued clockwise rotation of the defender on his vertical y-axis will probably result in the dislocation and/or separation of the attacker's parent joint (hip.)

By understanding and applying the four structural factors (common characteristics, consistent control movements, standard steps, and the effective use of joint-chain hierarchies), you will be well on your way to applying figure-4 locks more effectively. You will have built a strong and yet flexible framework within which you can better work toward the mastery of figure-4 locks. This knowledge is essential if you plan to fine-tune your technical skills, which you'll be able to do using the information presented in the next chapter.

Chapter 3
Finishing the House—
The Small Stuff Is Important

At this point, you have a sound foundation and a solid framework for setting up effective figure-4 locks. However, there is still room for some fine-tuning.

When I talk about the "small stuff," I'm referring to little details like proper hand or finger placement, footwork, body placement, turning your head to support the direction of your ki, just to name a few. They're the small movements that make any technique, especially figure-4 locks, more efficient and effective.

Often it's the small stuff that is ignored, either intentionally or out of ignorance. Some students, after much practice, discover some of the small stuff on their own. However, most never do because they're not looking for a key to make a figure-4 lock more effective or because they don't even know that they should.

But it is the small stuff that makes life easier. These details make figure-4 locks more effective and can guarantee you 100-percent success in many cases. Jujitsu students of mine who have honed their skills and use the "small stuff" have subdued real street attackers within a few (three to five) seconds. So don't let the phrase "small stuff" mislead you.

Unlike other instructors, I prefer to teach the small stuff to my students from the beginning. Why? Because it's easier to teach small stuff to new students and have them learn correctly from the outset. If students learn bad habits, it will take me more time later on to help them unlearn those bad habits. So let's get started.

Ki Flow

If you seriously study any martial art, or any sport for that matter, the issue of and the need for ki (proper energy flow) will eventually surface. It can't be ignored and shouldn't be because the proper use of ki is essential to maximizing your actions at the right time. This is why a lot of jujitsu holds and locks don't feel like anything until the last moment when they're set or executed. This is also why the locks and holds are set slowly in practice so a training partner can tap out before injury occurs.

Ki is like energy. In fact, it is your body's energy flow. A Western definition of energy flow would refer to it as the momentum your body creates when it moves in a certain direction. In simple scientific terms, momentum (ki) is equal to the mass of an object times its velocity in a given direction (p=m*v). (The formula can become far more complex, but this isn't a course in physics.) This momentum can even extend the energy of your movement beyond the body and into an innate object, i.e., if you are thrusting with a spear, stabbing with a knife, throwing a ball—any object.

The Eastern definition of energy flow looks at ki as a flowing current in your body. If your body or organs are out of alignment, your ki cannot "flow" properly. This concept also applies to your natural physical alignment of being balanced to carry out any physical movement. It is only when you are physically balanced that you can accept the energy flow of others and redirect it in a path that you desire.

There is an old rule in judo that applies to all the soft arts that use circular ki. Circular ki occurs when you are moving in a balanced circular direction and your energy flow is in that same direction. The rule states that the attacker's body will go in whatever direction his head is going for that is the direction of his ki. So, if your attacker's head moves or turns to his right, you can guide his ki in that direction, as well, thus causing him to move or fall toward his right.

There is, however, a much more important aspect to the proper use of ki. As stated before, your body must be balanced and able to easily move in the direction you want in order to effectively use your and your attacker's ki. This will also allow you to use consistent control movements to set up effective figure-4 locks.

However, the most critical element in the effective use of your ki is the ability to turn your head, body and extremities in the direction you want to go along your vertical y-axis. On the assumption that all your consistent control movements are in place and figure-4 locks on joints are set for execution, you MUST rotate on your y-axis AND you MUST turn your head in the direction you want to go.

In a class situation, most students tend to watch their attacker's facial expressions to see whether a technique is working. This is a natural thing to do. As humans, we're very sensitive to facial expressions. Facial expressions provide a lot of information about how a person feels. However, watching your attacker's face is counterproductive to executing any technique in any martial art. In the soft arts, watching your attacker's face will keep you from rotating on your y-axis. As a result, you will be unable to execute the technique you're trying to use. If you set up your techniques properly and turn your head in the direction you want to rotate rather than watching your attacker's face, the technique will work.

In jujitsu, the Eastern version of ki is absolutely essential to the success of most techniques. Yes, force can be used, but it is an inefficient use of energy that can be easily countered.

The proper alignment of your body and extremities will maximize your ki flow. Ki flows away from your body in the direction in which your body and your extremities are moving—right down to your fingertips. Your ki flow can either be in a straight line (less controllable) or in a circular direction (more controllable). The extension of ki in a circular direction is more controllable because the energy extended can be continuously supported by the ki flow in your body (from your "center"). Also, if your fingertips are pointing away from you, your ki will flow outward and away from you. If your fingers are curled and pointed back toward you, like in a fist or a claw, your ki will also be directed back toward you.

Straight Energy (*Ki*) Extension

This is an open-hand finger strike to the throat.

Energy can also be extended in a straight line with a hit by the defender's fist.

Circular Energy (*Ki*) Extension

This is a simple review of the basic hand throw.

It demonstrates the circular flow of *ki*.

With ki flow, the defender brings the attacker down.

You may be wondering how a discussion about figure-4 locks gets sidetracked by an explanation about ki flow. The answer is that the setup of all figure-4 locks is based on the natural flow of energy by the defender and the effective use of the energy extended by the attacker. Through the effective use of your attacker's energy flow, it is possible to quickly and easily move you and your attacker's extremities into a lock. Once set, any attempt by the attacker to resist the figure-4 lock will result in movement by the attacker in a direction directly opposite to the direction in which the attacker wishes to go.

Energy Flow vs. Resistance

In this picture, the basic figure-4 shoulder lock is set for execution. The attacker (left) attempts to move in the opposite direction of the defender's *ki* flow.

This causes his own ki flow to move in a direction opposite to the direction he wishes to go, proportionately supplementing the direction of energy flow of the actual shoulder lock and causing more effective execution of it.

This type of reaction occurs because the figure-4 lock has locked a parent joint. Any action by the attacker after this point will only off-balance the attacker more. In effect, a properly set figure-4 lock will result in an almost 100-percent efficient opposite movement by the attacker; momentum equals mass times velocity, remember? The attacker's momentum won't overcome the defender's ki flow, so he will move in the direction he doesn't want to go.

It might be possible to make an almost parallel argument for effectively delivered hits and kicks except that a certain amount of energy is lost in the impact. Once a figure-4 lock is properly set and the defender is totally committed to maintaining the hold, the defender requires no or very little additional energy output at this point. Any energy expended by the attacker to counter the lock is immediately redirected against him.

Hand Grip vs. Hook for Effective Leverage

Most of the time, if you tell a martial arts student (even a black belt) to grip another opponent's forearm or knee when executing a figure-4 lock, he'll grab it with his fingers on one side and his thumb on the opposing side. His grip is similar to how he'd grab a baseball bat. This is a natural thing to do. This is the natural grip he has used since birth. The student hasn't made a mistake. In his mind, a grip and a grab are the same thing.

Normal Hand-Grab Motion

direction of ki

neutralizes

direction of ki

This is a picture of a normal open hand "grab/grip." The fingers are on one side of the grip, and the opposing thumb is on the other. Notice that as the thumb and fingers need to squeeze against each other to maintain a grip/grab, the *ki* flow of one neutralizes the other, thus resulting in a weaker connection and weaker technique.

This picture shows setting up a wrist-lock lift submission using a normal grab/grip.

This is the wrist-lock lift set with a grab/grip. This is a fairly weak submission because it requires strength to maintain it because of the conflicting use of *ki* energy.

However, what you are really doing when you do a grab or grip is to "hook" your hand over the forearm or knee of the attacker so it acts as a brace in the figure-4 lock. You want the thumb and fingers next to each other, side by side, as shown in the following pictures.

Hooked Hands

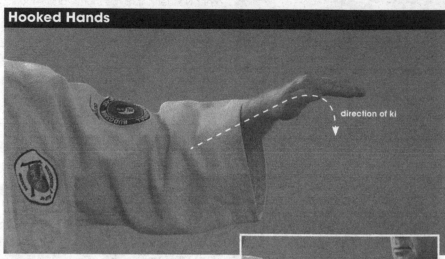

direction of ki

In this picture of a properly hooked hand, the fingers and thumb are aligned with each other, not opposing each other. In this way, all the *ki* directed through the defender's arm extends out through his wrist and hand and downward.

Notice how the defender's left hand is hooking over his right forearm. Setting a hold in this manner allows his arm, wrist and hand to operate more solidly as a single unit.

Hooked Hands Resting on the Forearm

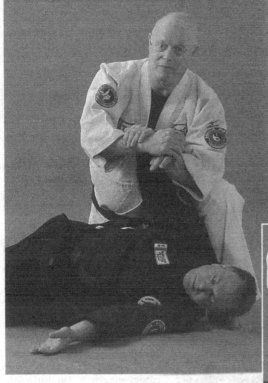

In this picture, the defender is setting up a wrist-lock lift submission with hooked hands.

This picture shows a close-up of the hook approach.

So what's the advantage of the "hook" verses the "grab"?

First, the hook preserves the straight line of the y-axis of the defender's forearm, hand, and fingers and thumb. By maintaining this straight line, the wrist of the defender is no longer a weak point in the y-axis. This allows the defender's forearm to act as a solid base for the figure-4 lock. As a result, it's also more difficult for the attacker to escape from a hook.

Proper Setup of a Figure-4 Wrist-Lock Lift Submission

In this picture, the defender is demonstrating the proper setup of a wrist-lock lift using hooked hands.

This close-up shows a proper figure-4 wrist-lock lift. Using hooked hands allows all *ki* to be directed against the back of attacker's hand and up the attacker's arm in line with the y-axis of his forearm.

hip thrust forces defender into upright position

direction of hip thrust

direction of ki

Once the wrist lock is set, all the defender needs to do to execute the submission is to thrust his hips forward slightly. This motion will straighten the defender up quickly—much faster than pulling up on the wrist press. This hip "thrust" results in upward pressure (*ki*) being applied to the back of the attacker's hand without any additional effort. It's a much more efficient way to execute the wrist-lock lift submission.

Second, using a hook allows the figure-4 lock to be set correctly and allows the submission to be executed through movement of the torso, usually at the center point of the x, y and z axes. If you grabbed an opponent naturally, ki-flow conflict created by the placement of opposing fingers and thumb weakens the wrist, creating a weak point in the y-axis at your wrist joint. This goes back to the concept of levers and pivot points: You can only have one pivot point in a technique, not two or three. No other joints in your body should be moving.

If, however, you are grabbing the forearm of your attacker with a grab, the opposing energy of your thumb and fingers turns all the finger and thumb joints plus the wrist into pivot points. All these pivot points destroy the integral strength of your arm's y-axis because your effort is being used to maintain the grip on the attacker's forearm rather than properly executing the figure-4 lock. With no effective base, the figure-4 lock is significantly weakened and can be more easily countered.

Pronation vs. Supination

There are two ways to rotate an extremity: either inward, toward the body (pronation), or outward, away from the body (supination). There are strengths and weaknesses to both.

When using pronation, joint rotation will occur inwardly, toward the attacker's body. This, in turn, implements a joint-chain hierarchy in which the parent joint, like the shoulder, locks first, forcing the attacker's torso to bend forward at his humanoid joint (the sacrum). The advantage of pronation is that it's easier to do and doesn't require as much skill as supination. This is because there are fewer steps to setting up a figure-4 lock when using pronation. The second advantage of pronation is that as a martial artist, skilled in jujitsu, *aikijitsu* or *aikido*, you can easily bend the attacker's joint inward and perpendicular to the y-axis of the attacker's extremity that is being turned.

The weakness of simply twisting a joint in an inward direction is that it allows the attacker to maintain the integrity of the parent joint's y-axis for a longer period. If the attacker can maintain the integrity of the y-axis, which is being twisted, he has a better chance of maintaining the y-axis of his torso and escaping the technique if the figure-4 lock is not set up correctly. For the attacker, maintaining the integrity of the y-axis (even though the defender has twisted it) makes it possible for the attacker to counter the defender's technique and balance himself. He wants to extend his ki through the y-axis of the rotated parent joint before any lock is set.

Once the defender destroys the integrity of the y-axis of the attacker's extremity using pronation, then the attacker's options are far more limited—if he has any at all—because the y-axis of his torso will be destroyed, as well.

Straight Energy (*Ki*) Extension

Both the defender (right) and the attacker are in a ready position.

The attacker strikes with an overhead club. The defender cross-blocks.

The defender deflects the blow to his right, thus directing the movement of the attacker's right arm inward, toward his body (pronation).

The defender then rotates the attacker's arm down, ...

...changing his block into a double wrist grab (loose C-grip) as he brings his arm down the rest of the way.

A C-grip is a loose grip around the attacker's wrist with the thumb and index finger of both hands.

Note: A loose C-grip is used during practice to avoid sudden or cumulative injury to the attacker's shoulder.

The defender steps in with his right foot, beyond the attacker, while he grips the wrist of the attacker tightly.

Note: Keep the C-grip loose in practice to avoid severe shoulder injury to your attacker. The attacker, in turn, will do a nice forward roll for you.

Continued ▶

The defender rotates counterclockwise (to his left) as he brings the arm of the attacker up and over his head. "On the street," the attacker's arm has now been twisted counterclockwise to lock the shoulder (parent joint) and then the elbow (child joint) of the arm (corkscrew) toward the torso—pronation—and the defender is ready to execute the throw.

The defender now directs the locked arm of the attacker forward in the same direction ...

... and then down in a circular motion, ...

... guiding the attacker through the throw.

In the *dojo*, the attacker should be able to execute a forward roll and land on his back.

On the street, the attacker will usually land on his head and/or right shoulder, resulting in severe trauma to either or both areas.

Supination also has its strengths and weaknesses. The downside of supination and figure-4 locks is that they are more complicated and require greater skill because they have more steps that must be completed in a specific order. However, the major strength of supination is that it lends itself much more easily to the setting up and execution of a greater variety of figure-4 locks, its figure-4 locks are more effective, and the attacker will probably not realize that a figure-4 lock has been set until it's too late for him to react effectively or counter it.

By turning an extremity outward (supination), you lock all the joints in the joint-chain hierarchy of an extremity in sequential order. For example, if you rotate the wrist outward, the elbow and shoulder (parent joint) will follow. From this point, the attacker's back will arch backward at the humanoid joint, also destroying the body's y-axis. With the figure-4 lock secure, the defender can throw the opponent, execute a takedown, or finish with a standing submission or submission on the ground. The most common/severe injury to the extremity will probably occur to the parent joint when the technique is effectively executed. There may also be serious injuries to other parts of the assailant from his impact with the ground.

It is also important to note that, if the lock is properly set, additional movement of the defender's arms and hands should be unnecessary. The defender's torso and accompanying footwork does the finishing work. Any resistance by the attacker will only quicken the execution of the figure-4 lock.

Reverse Corkscrew to Shoulder-Lock Rear Takedown Showing Supination

The attacker (right) strikes the defender with an overhead club. The defender executes a cross-block, ...

... deflecting the club attack to his left.

He continues the counterclockwise motion of his deflection in a downward and counterclockwise circle.

The defender then brings the attacker's arm back up, continuing the counterclockwise circle when he starts to set a C-grip on the attacker's right wrist.

Note: The C-grip is kept relatively loose so that the attacker doesn't know what will happen next.

Continued

As he brings the attacker's arm up, ...

... the defender squats slightly (if necessary) while rotating clockwise and turning to the attacker's right.

Now the defender is facing the opposite direction of the attacker.

To finish the shoulder-lock rear takedown, all the defender needs to do is continue the counterclockwise movement of the attacker's arm, setting the C-grip. He brings the attacker's arm downward and to the attacker's rear.

Note: Extreme caution should be used in executing this technique in the *dojo*. Allow the attacker to fall backward on his own. Pull his arm only enough to guide him down. Otherwise you run the risk of dislocating and/or separating his shoulder, which are both serious injuries.

Alternative Ending to Reverse Corkscrew Into a Shoulder-Lock Comealong

As an alternative, the defender can go into a rear shoulder-lock comealong by continuing his clockwise turn. He turns into the attacker from behind his opponent.

As the defender turns in, his left hand lets go of his C-grip ...

... and reaches around to hook under the attacker's upper arm, pulling it back to keep him off-balance.

The defender moves his right C-grip down on the attacker's wrist so his palm can rest on the back of his hand and bend it. The defender secures the grip at this point. He can control the attacker by rotating his hand left or right, thus locking his wrist joint. Be careful because you can create quite a bit of pain extremely fast if this control is set up properly.

Note: The detail picture shows a lot of space between the attacker and the defender. This was done so you can see the wrist lock. Normally, you would be as close to the attacker as possible. Otherwise, the attacker might be able to turn out of this shoulder-lock comealong before it's set.

The defender moves the attacker's left forearm so that it is resting against the back or right rear side of the attacker's neck. This sets a foundation for the comealong. Once this comealong is set, the defender can move the attacker in almost any direction by winding the attacker's right hand left or right at the attacker's wrist as necessary. The defender can then walk the attacker in any direction he wishes or use the attacker as a shield against other potential assailants.

Another reason to show pronation and supination techniques together is to illustrate a forgiving nature of jujitsu. The forward corkscrew (*mae ude guruma*) requires that you turn your body to your left (counterclockwise) while turning the attacker's arm inward—pronation. The reverse cork-screw to shoulder-lock rear takedown (*ude guruma ushiro*) requires that you turn your body to your right (clockwise) while turning the attacker's arm outward—supination. The movements of both these techniques are identical except that they start with the defender turning in opposite directions. The forgiving nature of jujitsu is that whatever direction you turn in setting up a defensive technique, you will end up with a viable technique—usually one that includes a figure-4 lock.

For that reason, a good *sensei*, if he sees his student starting a technique by turning in the opposite direction, will tell him to keep on moving but go slowly. There are no second chances on the street. If you start doing something backward, you can't ask your attacker on the street to start over again. You only get one chance. If you know your techniques, you'll automatically set up a viable one and end up "helping" your attacker go in whatever direction he or you choose to go.

Foot and Torso Placement

If you think repetitive footwork and *kata* are limited to the traditional martial arts, "you ain't been out of the barn." Proper footwork, body form, natural movement and alignment are essential to success in any physical activity. [Footwork is essential because it keeps you balanced on your axes and your body in the right place for whatever action you plan to take.]

Proper footwork and torso placement of the defender is absolutely essential for any ground submission, especially figure-4 locks. Even a slight amount of space between the defender and the attacker or a misalignment of the defender's torso or feet can create a major eight-lane highway for the attacker's escape. I call this space "crotch space" because it's most evident in the space between the defender's crotch and the attacker's shoulder when the defender attempts to set a figure-4 armbar or wrist-lock lift submission on the ground. Many times, the defender will attempt a butt-scoot (sounds like a line-dancing step), or he'll pull on the attacker's arm to compensate. Both these are poor remedies because they support counters/reversals by the attacker.

Poorly set figure-4 locks, in which there is space between the attacker and the defender, can result in the defender being easily off-balanced. They also allow the attacker to easily escape or counter the defender's techniques. The photo sequences that follow show a few simple counters for poorly set locks on the ground in which there is crotch space between you and the attacker. These are relatively easy escapes but should be practiced slowly for safety's sake.

Armbar Escape and Counter

Crotch space is caused by the defender setting up a wrist-lock lift or figure-4 armbar while the attacker is flat on his back. Note the amount of space between the defender's crotch and the right shoulder of the attacker. It's impossible to set either of the holds properly if the attacker is on his back.

For example, one easy and effective counter is for the attacker to reach or "shoot" through the unset figure-4 armbar with his right arm, bending it over the defender's upper arm (thus breaking the figure-4) while his left hand reaches up and grabs the defender's left shoulder.

Notice how the defender is off-balanced by this counter.

The attacker immediately traps the defender's left arm close to his own body and turns to his left. He rotates his own y-axis to take the defender over him and set for a reverse armbar.

The attacker can also hook onto his own hand with his left hand and roll the defender over him and continue as before, rotating his own y-axis to take the defender over him and set for a reverse armbar.

Wrist-Lock Lift Escape

An improperly set wrist-lock lift can be easily countered by

... the attacker (bottom) reaching over with his left hand and grabbing his right elbow (same concept as for countering an armbar) ...

... and then trapping the defender's right forearm. He holds it close to his chest while rolling to his left on his own y-axis.

This rolls the defender over the attacker.

Note: The attacker holds you as close to his body as possible because the closer the attacker can get you to his y-axis, the easier it will be for him to successfully rotate on his y-axis.

Punching the Wrist Press

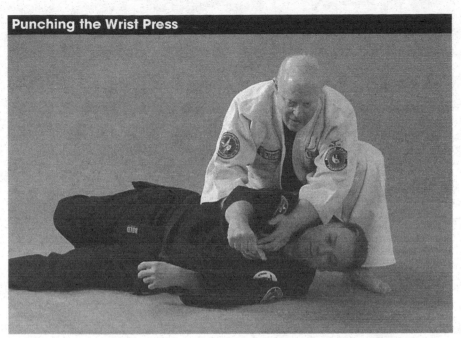

Another counter option for the attacker (bottom) is to make a fist with his right hand (to protect his wrist) and then turn to his left as he punches or shoots through the poorly set wrist press. If the attacker can turn to his left, he can release the pressure on the back of his hand because his turn will off-balance the defender for a moment.

The next sequence (on page 76) provides some examples of how to prevent crotch space as you set up figure-4 locks. Your goal should always be to set any hold or lock as tightly as possible and as close to the attacker as possible. Any space between you and your attacker or any gaps in a lock or hold will give your attacker the ability to move. If your attacker has the ability to move, he can gain flexibility and eventually a base by which to effectively counter you. You don't want to give him that opportunity. The following examples should help you prevent crotch space, thus resulting in quicker and more effective figure-4 lock submissions. It's always easier to prevent a problem than to try to fix it after the fact.

Preventing Crotch Space

There are several things the defender (top) can do to prevent crotch space or the room to give the attacker the opportunity to counter. First, and most important, is to make sure the attacker lands on his left side, with his back to the defender. If the defender can keep the attacker on his left side, the attacker's other extremities can't reach him.

Whether it is for an armbar or a wrist-lock lift, the defender makes sure his right knee is against the attacker's back and his left ankle/instep is against the back of the defender's head. The defender's left foot can be partially under the attacker's head or neck. This will keep him from turning toward the defender.

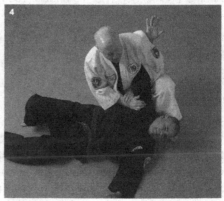

This will allow the defender to place his knee on the side of the attacker's head—preferably in a line from his ear/temple to his nose and shift the defender's body weight onto his left knee, if the attacker resists in any way.

Note: Be careful when practicing this because it is a multiple-nerve attack and can be very painful for the attacker. It also creates a better base position if you choose to execute the wrist-lock lift or arm bar because it will keep the attacker's body pinned to the ground. Again, there is no "crotch space" when the hold is set.

Another option from this position (left knee against the back of attacker's head) is for the defender to maintain the armbar and simply roll back onto his back. His left knee should keep the attacker's head and torso in place. The defender executes the back roll carefully to avoid dislocating the attacker's elbow, or, if he's doing a wrist-lock lift, from breaking his wrist.

Another option for the defender is to place his left foot in front of the attacker's neck, under his chin.

Note: This will reduce the chance of him biting the back of your leg.

If the defender senses any resistance or countering, he can simply roll back, set a scissor with his legs around the attacker's neck and automatically execute the arm bar or wrist-lock lift submission. Notice that there's an absolute lack of "crotch space" here. If the defender rolls back, the attacker's neck will be scissored just below his crotch; that's far more effective than being scissored at the knee joints.

If the defender's left leg is in front of the attacker's neck, under his chin, the defender can also fall back while his left leg keeps the attacker's head in place. This is actually a little safer than the rollback in the previous caption.

Note: Keep in mind that self-defense and competing on the mat in a *dojo* or in formal competition (*randori*) are two entirely different situations. In a street situation, the immediate goal of any lock is to cause sufficient pain or injury to end the altercation so you can get away safely. In randori, you can take your time.

The above sequence illustrates your options once you have a knee down on the ground. However, just because you've put the attacker down on his left side does not mean you have to go down onto one knee (to brace against his back). If your intention is to immediately go into a submission on the ground, particularly if you're using any type of armbar, wrist press or wrist-lock lift, there are two far more efficient and much faster ways to set up your submission position; although, they have a bit more risk for you. The double knee brace is simple enough to require only one picture. However, in practice, you and your attacker need to cooperate fully to prevent him from being injured because this trapping position occurs extremely fast. Even if done slowly, it will lift your attacker off the ground because of the unexpected speed of the trap and the momentum of your torso rolling back. The double knee brace is a great example of a first-class lever.

Double Knee Brace

Once the attacker is thrown and is on his left side, the defender rolls him forward slightly. He rolls the attacker with his knees when the he starts to bend them. Once the defender has a secure fit (knees bent and tight against the attacker), he simply rolls back. The attacker will be tight against the defender's knees, and the lock will be extremely secure.

Note: Rolling back may literally lift the attacker off the ground, set whatever lock you have, and it will result in severe joint injury to the attacker. In practice, you will probably have to relax your hold on whatever lock you use to avoid injury to the attacker.

The double leg pin follows the same concept as the double knee brace. Its downside is that it's not set up as fast as the double knee brace. Its advantage is that it's more controllable and that its steps can be more easily visualized.

Double Leg Pin

Once the attacker is down and is on his left side, the defender's right foot steps over the attacker's body. The defender must make sure to lean forward a bit when he pulls the attacker's trapped arm. He wants the attacker's right arm to be about 45 degrees from the ground. If he steps over with his left foot first, that's OK, too.

The defender brings his left foot over when he sits down on the back of the attacker's right shoulder and upper torso (front side of ribs). He should feel that he's sitting on the attacker's shoulder/ribs. There should be no crotch space.

The defender rolls back onto the ground. If the defender is holding onto the lock (arm-bar, shoulder lock, wrist-lock lift, wrist press) tightly, he will literally lift the attacker off the ground because of the tightness of this trap.

When the attacker comes down, the defender makes sure that both his legs are firmly against his torso so he can bring the attacker down "hard."

Continued ➡

The defender maintains a hold of whatever he has (an armbar in this example) and leans back to submit.

If the defender loses the armbar in the process of executing the trap, which is not uncommon, he does not waste his time trying to reset the hold. He simply rotates his left arm over the attacker's arm in a counterclockwise direction and latches it under the outside of his own left leg as high as possible. The defender then leans back. This will set a strong enough armbar to dislocate the attacker's elbow, if the defender desires to do so.

Admittedly, crotch space is a blunt term to use. However, it is accurate and students pick up the concept quickly. Crotch space has become a common term that means the defender needs to check for any spaces between his attacker and himself or any misalignment of his feet or torso that would create an opening for his attacker to use for escape. The crotch-space concept also forces the defender to check his x-y-z alignment with his attacker. The axes need to be parallel or perpendicular to each other (and sometimes at a 45-degree angle—between the head and shoulder of the attacker), dependent on the technique being used, so that the technique can be done efficiently. The photo sequences on pages 81 to 85 show perpendicular, parallel and 45-degree alignment examples.

Perpendicular Alignment Examples

Armbar—on the ground

Armbar—standing

Wrist-Lock Press—standing

Wrist-Lock Wind—standing

Continued

Leg-Lock Lift

Figure-4 Leg Brace—on the ground

Head Lock—on the ground

Parallel Alignment Examples

Shoulder Lock—standing

Shoulder Lock—on the ground

Arm Trap With Key Turn—on the ground

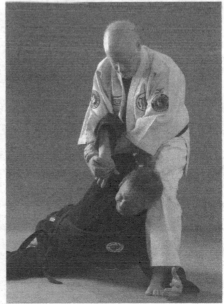

Wrist-Lock Lift

Continued

Rear-Carotid Submission

Wrist-Lock Lift (*Koga* Comealong)

Wrist-Press Lift—on the ground

Figure-4 Leg Lock—ground

45-Degree Alignment Examples

Wrist Press—on the ground   Wrist-Lock Lift With Head Trap—on the ground

Keep Hold of the Extremity: Resistance Is Futile

There is nothing more effective than a well-set figure-4 lock, maintained to cause different levels of pain (in order to secure cooperation—aka "compliance" in the law-enforcement community) or quickly break or dislocate a joint, if necessary. In the past few years, I have had an increasing number of students who have come to me with a limited amount of mixed-martial arts training who have been taught to constantly change holds while grabbing. However, I doubt any good instructor would teach his students to let go of a perfectly good lock to go into another hold. But I've seen this happen time and time again. It may be that the MMA student who comes into my *dojo* doesn't believe in the effectiveness of simple joint locks as compared to what he has been taught. Or it may be that the student really believes he has to grapple around on the ground as part of the submission process (although "chicken-scratch" situations can occur on the street).

One of the rules Seki ground into me was that, if you had hold of an extremity, then you don't let go of it. If you used a joint torque or figure-4 lock for a throw and you still have a hold of it after the opponent is down, use it for a submission. One thing I do with grappling students is get them into a wrist-lock press with their elbow on the ground. I then ask them to get out of the submission. Although they have free use of their other extremities (plus they could flip their bodies), they can't escape. This is possible because the press is set properly—my body and feet were properly placed and axes aligned. And, most important, because of my correct body alignment, I am able to control the level of pain in the wrist press. There's also the additional factor that the purpose of the wrist press is to break the wrist *and* that a properly set wrist press can cause a lot of pain (for control/compliance purposes) before the joint actually fractures.

Admittedly, traditional *jujitsu* makes ample use of small joints and joint-dampening beyond sport judo and MMA competition, but that's because traditional jujitsu is oriented around self-defense, not competition. Also, traditional jujitsu teaches many types of figure-4 locks for various situations and from different positions. This knowledge is a tremendous asset on the street.

Another advantage of understanding the kinesthetics of joint movement and joint dampening is to help your attacker rather than fight him if he's resisting a lock that you're trying to set. Oftentimes, going with your attacker's movement actually allows you to set up another figure-4 lock. The ability to execute this skill allows you to "help" your attacker into a more secure position (at least for you). Once a lock is properly set, he will then learn that resistance is futile. Any resistance on his part will create a proportionately increased level of pain and discomfort.

For example, I am in the process of setting an armbar submission on my opponent (with both of us on the ground and my back against his side). I sense resistance because my opponent wants to bend his elbow to get out of the armbar. I'll simply allow him to do so, turning my body to my right and toward his head along my y-axis if I'm on the ground, or I'll turn counterclockwise to my left on my perpendicular y-axis if I'm kneeling next to him. This changes the armbar into a shoulder lock, which my opponent has helped me set. That's why Seki often said, "Help your opponent. Don't fight him." There's also a philosophical issue here in that helping your opponent rather than fighting him complements the martial artist's philosophy of nonviolence.

Armbar Switch to Shoulder Lock (Kneeling at His Right Side)

The defender starts to set a figure-4 armbar with the attacker's hands/arms.

However, the attacker manages to bend his trapped right arm (for whatever reason—probably the defender's leg was in front of his head, which gave him crotch space to move).

The defender immediately gets his left leg behind the attacker's head to reduce his opponent's maneuvering ability. He allows the attacker to bend his right arm completely so his elbow is up and his hand and shoulder are down. The defender makes sure his right hand is now resting on the attacker's chest, which he is pushing down.

The defender rotates his forearm counter-clockwise along the y-axis of the attacker's upper arm. The defender does this by rotating his own body to the left along his own torso's y-axis. This will dampen the attacker's shoulder joint and set the figure-4 shoulder lock.

Armbar Switch to Shoulder-Lock Submission Showing Supination

The defender starts to set a figure-4 armbar while lying at the attacker's right side. If he is unable to hook onto the attacker's right arm with his right hand, it is acceptable to grab his own *gi* or even his belt.

The attacker bends his trapped arm.

But the defender turns toward the attacker's head, helping the attacker bend his right arm.

Continuing to turn, the defender pulls the attacker's wrist, with his palm up, toward himself. This sets up a wrist press.

The defender wants to pull the attacker's wrist into him as much as possible. His chest pushes on the attacker's elbow from his elbow's underside. This will set the shoulder lock and wrist press at the same time. This is shown more clearly in the insert.

Figure-4 Shoulder Lock With the Leg

To set up a figure-4 shoulder lock, the defender uses his legs if, when trying to set up an armbar, the attacker bends his right arm.

The defender brings his right leg up and over the attacker's arm, allowing and helping the attacker bend his arm.

The attacker bends his arm around the defender's leg, which is what the defender wants.

The defender brings his leg down...

... as he turns his body toward the attacker's head to keep the attacker's head and torso down.

At this point, the defender can straighten his right leg very slowly to execute a shoulder lock on the attacker.

Note: In practice, do this very slowly because your leg muscles are extremely strong. You'll also notice that I've set a head lock to enhance the body pin.

The defender can also enhance the submission by setting the head lock on the back of the attacker's head (rather than neck) and then pulling his head into his chest.

Note: Execute this head lock pin very slowly for a variety of safety reasons but mostly to protect the attacker's neck vertebrae from serious injury.

Chapter 4
The Street and the Dojo—
A Sense of Direction

The purpose of presenting the background information and theory to all figure-4 locks is to provide you with common and consistent tools that will make figure-4 locks easier to set up. It will also make them more effective in kata and self-defense situations. In terms of jujitsu kata, developing the skills to automatically and correctly set up figure-4 locks is as important as learning proper distraction techniques (hits, nerve attacks, releases), actual techniques (throws, reverses, submissions, comealongs), and finishing techniques (joint-lock submissions, pins, hits and kicks, chokes and strangulations, and other submissions). The constant kata practice establishes muscle memory and trains your mind so you can move automatically on the street, using *mushin* rather than conscious thought.

You also have to realize that what you can do on the mat and what you can do on the street are two different things. On the mat, your goal is to secure a submission from your opponent, not to injure him. This tends to involve the use of the parent joints (which won't succumb to joint injuries as quickly as child joints) and your body mass to hold your opponent down. Although there is still a chance of joint injury, your attacker can usually tap out before serious injury.

The street is a different scenario. You have a twofold goal: to prevent any further physical attack on yourself and to safely remove yourself from the current situation and environment. In doing so, you may simply be able to control your assailant or you may be left with no other choice except to seriously and perhaps permanently disable him. Consequences for your attacker are usually determined by the situation and your perception of the situation, especially if you're "in fear for your life." Figure-4 locks, especially if applied to child joints in a street situation, can be quickly and easily executed, bringing a conflict to a quick ending through the creation of a great deal of controlled pain, fracture or joint dislocation for your attacker anywhere along the joint-chain hierarchy.

If you are a member of a law-enforcement agency and you are acting within your agency's use-of-force policy, your goal is not to injure the other party but only to secure compliance, unless injury is absolutely necessary and justifiable. There's a twofold advantage to this approach. First, from a martial artist's philosophical point of view, you are supporting the concept of nonviolence as much as possible. A physical confrontation is the most degrading action a martial artist can be in. It indicates that all rational means of resolving a conflict have failed. By ending a physical conflict without injuring your opponent at least serves to show that you were able to uphold the philosophical concepts of your martial art with respect to nonviolence.

Second, which runs concurrently with the first advantage, once a figure-4 lock is set properly, there will be no pain or discomfort to the attacker unless he chooses to be noncompliant. Then, the more noncompliant he is, the more painful the lock becomes, eventually resulting in greater pain, discomfort and/or injury caused by the attacker and not by your use of strength or force.

If, however, you're in fear for your life and there's no other alternative, you might be justified in quickly applying sufficient leverage or torque to sprain, break and/or dislocate a child and/or parent joint or fracture an extremity bone by using a figure-4 lock.

If you apply figure-4 locks properly, effectively implementing the characteristics described in the first three chapters of this book, you will be able to more successfully defend yourself either from a distance (length of the attacker's arm or leg), using the attacker's child joints, or at close range, using parent joints The situation will determine whether you use a comealong or standing submission, bring your opponent down to the ground with a control hold, or use leverage and/or joint-locking techniques to actually throw your opponent to the ground. Figure-4 locks can be used in any of these situations and most likely will be an integral part of whatever self-defense techniques you use. Your goal in defending yourself is to remove yourself from the situation and minimize injury to yourself in the process. Effective use of figure-4 locks will help make that possible.

PART TWO

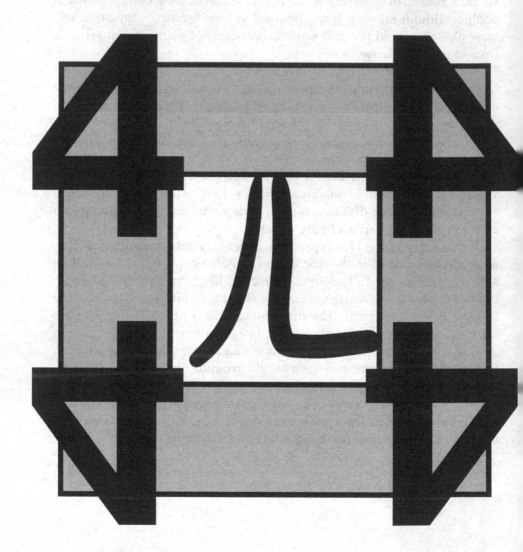

Chapter 5
Figure-4 Locks

The purpose of this chapter is to present actual techniques (and some variations) that apply the previously presented theories. I will not be showing every lock or hold that I know because that would undermine the purpose of this book: to learn the basic concepts of figure-4 locks and then apply those concepts to situations you find yourself in on the mat.

The Japanese names for these techniques were created by Seki, my jujitsu sensei. The names use generic terminology, but they are not always consistent.

Second, the phonetic spelling of the Japanese terminology may not be consistent with other Japanese words. Although I have attempted to use generic spelling whenever possible, there are some alternative spellings. Because the translation is from Japanese to English, there may be many cases in which there is no definitive spelling for a Japanese word, term or phrase.

Third, the English name for the technique is kept generic whenever possible. In the long run, using generic terminology makes it easier to remember each technique because the names (Japanese or English) reflect the movements made by the defender or attacker. This creates a certain amount of consistency in the learning process. Surprisingly, the generic Japanese terms make more sense than the English ones because Japanese terms are all-encompassing.

Finally, different *ryu* of jujitsu sometimes use different names for the same basic techniques. This only adds to the Pandora's box with respect to language. Despite all this, the variations of Japanese names are still far more consistent than the English translations for traditional jujitsu techniques.

Returning to the actual techniques in this section, I will continue to deal with the "small stuff." This will help keep you from making mistakes. Even if you do make errors, hopefully you will have the skills to recover by the time you have mastered the figure-4 techniques and concepts presented in this book.

A Serious Word of Caution!

Figure-4 submissions, whether they're called holds, locks, submissions, pins or comealongs, are designed to cause serious physical injury to an assailant: usually a joint dislocation and/or separation to one or more joints along the joint-chain hierarchy. They may also cause serious injuries to other parts of the body from hitting the ground or other solid objects. (As I tell my students, no one gets hurt falling, they get hurt when they hit an immovable object or the ground.) Therefore, it is absolutely essential that you, as the defender, practice these techniques slowly and correctly. If you are going to follow through on a throw, it is also absolutely necessary that you not move at a speed greater than your partner's ability as he is being thrown or falling. In essence, you must let him guide you for his own personal safety. Lastly, if you feel that your partner is resisting your technique, use good judgment and release the hold immediately. In most cases, there is a very fine line between resistance and injury.

It is also important that you know the difference between a comealong, takedown and throws because all of them are covered in this book. A comealong is a hold or lock, usually a figure-4, that you place on the attacker to secure his cooperation through pain compliance. Comealongs, from the term "come along with me," are used to move a person from one place to another. A comealong is different from a throw because it allows the defender to establish control over the attacker, who has both his feet on the ground at all times during the technique. Comealongs also allow you to use one attacker as a shield or buffer against other attackers or create an illusion of sufficient pain in the controlled attacker so that the other attackers will hopefully abandon the assault. An effectively set figure-4 lock comealong has the least chance of causing injury to your attacker unless he remains resistant. It also offers you the best control of your attacker.

A takedown occurs when the defender places the attacker in a lock or hold and brings him to the ground in a controlled manner. Most involve the use of figure-4 locks. One or both of the attacker's feet remain on the ground throughout the takedown. A takedown may be finished off with a submission. The level of injury caused by an effectively set figure-4 lock takedown can range from no injury at all (if you bring the attacker down slowly) to serious impact and joint dislocation, depending on how much the attacker resists and how quickly he is taken down.

A throw occurs when the defender uses any combination of the attacker's ki and momentum in combination with your own leverage, locks or holds to force the attacker's feet into the air as the technique is executed. If necessary, a throw can be finished off with a submission. A throw has the highest potential to injure the attacker, depending on the kind and speed of the throw, and the level of impact when he hits the ground. If you put the attacker down gently (just to "impress" him), there may be no injury at all. However, executing a throw at normal speed can cause serious concussions, bone fractures and dislocations primarily because most attackers don't know how to land safely. Many times a ground submission will not be necessary because of the damage caused by the throw.

Also, be aware that there is a working relationship between a comealong, takedown and a throw. A comealong may become a takedown or throw at your discretion. A takedown may become a throw if executed quickly. In some cases, a submission hold on the ground (or even with the attacker standing) can sometimes be converted to a comealong, depending on how well the lock is set and the situation you are in. Understanding the differences between comealongs, takedowns and throws can significantly affect the effectiveness of figure-4 locks and your control of your attacker.

As the attacker, it is absolutely essential that you use good judgment to protect yourself from immediate as well as cumulative joint injury that can result from several years of abusing your body. If you feel that a hold is set properly, tap the defender quickly and definitively or say *"maitte"* in a loud, clear voice. If you feel pain, tap the defender quickly and definitively or say *"maitte"* in a loud, clear voice. You're not trying to prove anything here except that you're a good attacker. Figure-4 submissions are designed to cause serious injury very quickly, so there is a very fine line between that and a set figure-4 lock. Tapping out also lets the defender know that he has applied enough pressure to control you (which is more important than dislocating your shoulder). If the defender learns how much pressure is needed to secure control or submit his opponent, he will have more control of his techniques on the street.

It is also important that you practice these techniques on each other with restraint. This will help you develop a sensitivity to your attacker's body movement as you set the hold. You will learn how to feel when you are at that submission point (at which parent joints have been fully torqued and dampened)—and injury will occur if any more leverage or pressure is applied. Once you develop this sensitivity, you will be more effective at controlling your attacker. You'll also have greater control over whether you injure your attacker rather than putting yourself in an all-or-nothing situation. Instead of you injuring the attacker, the attacker will injure himself if he chooses to resist a well-set figure-4 hold.

These are the reasons you must use caution during practice. In addition to learning effective submissions, you are also developing self-control and sensitivity to your opponent's body movements. Both these skills may help you if you have to deal with the legal system after defending yourself.

Lastly, there are some techniques presented in this book that simply cannot be executed without an extremely high or 100-percent risk of injury to your training partner. Do not attempt to complete techniques that have this warning. Please take all warnings and cautions seriously. Budoshin jujitsu is an extremely safe art to practice when you follow the safety rules and are considerate of your partner. It is also extremely street effective if it has to be used in self-defense.

Note: *Some of the techniques presented have numbers after their names. The numbers cross-reference my original notes found in Budoshin Jujitsu, 6th edition, (aka the "Big Book"), which contains more than 850 techniques and variations in the art. Some techniques do not have numbers simply because they aren't in the "Big Book." Perhaps if I do a 7th edition, I'll add them in.*

Armbars and Arm Locks

Winding Armbar with an Armbar Submission (*Gyaku Waza Makikomi*) 47

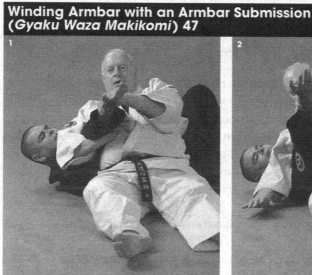

The defender is at the attacker's right side after the winding armbar throw and is ready to set up an armbar on the attacker. The submission is a basic figure-4 armbar used for a pin.

The defender leans as low as possible against the attacker's chest on the right side. The defender wraps his right arm over and under ...

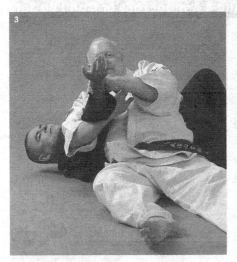

... the attacker's right arm (counterclockwise) at the attacker's elbow or just below the attacker's elbow.

The defender grabs his own left sleeve, *gi* lapel, belt, or pant leg (with his right hand) to hold the attacker's arm securely against the defender's right leg. The defender makes sure that he has a strong hook on the attacker's wrist. The defender's left hand is palm-down, and the attacker's arm is facing up.

The defender pushes down with his left hand to execute an armbar on the attacker.

Note: Do this carefully to avoid dislocating the attacker's elbow.

Armbar Wind Submission
(*Ude Makikomi*) 83—When a Figure-4 Armbar Fails or Can't Be Set

Ideally, the defender is facing the attacker on the attacker's right side and kneeling down. The defender's left knee is up, and his right knee is down after the throw. Also, notice that the y-axis of the attacker's right arm is parallel to the y-axis of the defender's body.

If the defender comes down on his left knee, the defender is at a 45-degree angle to the attacker, which creates a lot of crotch space for the attacker to maneuver.

If the defender attempts to set up an armbar on his own right side, most of the defender's body mass will be within the attacker's area of control.

The attacker can turn into the defender, pulling the defender down and off-balance.

The attacker grabs the defender's right shoulder, …

… and the attacker can pull the defender over him to the attacker's left.

If the defender keeps his right upper leg against the attacker's back and his left shin tight against the back of attacker's head, the attacker will have significantly less chance of escape. Setting the armbar on the defender's left side keeps most of the defender's body on the outside of the attacker's sphere of control.

Figure-4 Brace (*Ude Guruma*)

This is a relatively easy submission for the defender to set and maintain. The key is where the defender's left foot ends up.

The defender's left foot steps over the attacker's head and comes down in front of the attacker's face and under his chin.

As the defender rolls back, the defender's right knee, which is on the ground, rotates clockwise so that the defender's right foot is ideally resting against the back or right side of the attacker's head. The defender needs to make sure that his left forearm is under the attacker's trapped right arm.

The defender's left foot turns inward and goes under the attacker's left shoulder as much as possible. (See insert.) This will maintain the pin even if the attacker's elbow turns (as in this sequence) and the arm trap is slightly weakened. The close-up shows the defender's left foot under the attacker's left shoulder. Once this is set, little or no effort is necessary to maintain it.

Figure-4 Brace Variation (*Ude Guruma*)

The defender brings his right leg up and rests his lower leg across the front of the attacker's shoulder joint. The defender's right foot should be just above the attacker's shoulder and in front of his shoulder joint.

While the defender sets the armbar, the defender's left leg goes over his own right instep and hooks under the attacker's left shoulder. If the attacker has rotated his elbow to counter the armbar, the defender can still maintain the pin as long as he continues to control the attacker's right arm.

Rotating Rear Shoulder Lock (*Ude Guruma Ushiro*)

This is a great counter if the attacker (bottom) bends his elbow while the defender is setting a figure-4 armbar (*ude makikomi*) and …

… the attacker bends his right elbow to get out of the armbar.

The defender lets the attacker completely bend his elbow. The defender's right hand slides down from the attacker's shoulder to rest squarely on the attacker's right upper chest as the attacker bends his arm.

The defender then pushes down on the attacker's chest to get the attacker's right shoulder onto the ground as the defender's left hand slides down to provide additional downward pressure on the attacker's chest. The defender should make sure that his left knee (instep) is against the back of the attacker's head, thus limiting the attacker's mobility.

While maintaining strong downward pressure on the attacker's chest, the defender straightens his own body by thrusting his hips toward the attacker's shoulder, along his own z-axis, and turns to his left by rotating on his own y-axis. This will lock the attacker's shoulder, setting a rotating rear shoulder lock (*ude guruma ushiro*) and ultimately result in a severe shoulder injury.

Note: Use caution when executing!

Standing Rear Arm Lock (*Ude Guruma*) 760—for a Hit

The defender and the attacker face each other in a ready position.

The defender's left hand slides down and C-grips the attacker's right wrist. The defender does not need to grab the attacker's right wrist tightly. The defender's right forearm rests against the attacker's right upper arm so the defender can raise the attacker's arm up slightly as the defender ...

... goes under the attacker's right arm while the defender steps forward with his right foot.

Once the defender gets behind and to the right of the attacker, ...

... the defender's right arm goes in between the attacker's right upper arm and his back.

The defender continues this motion with his own right arm as the defender's left hand brings the attacker's arm up behind him.

Here is the same action from the front view.

The defender's right hand slips up and hooks onto the back of the attacker's right hand, ...

Continued

... which bends his hand inward (his fingers ideally pointing up) and sets a wrist press ...

... so the defender can set a proper arm-lock with a wrist press on the attacker. The defender needs to make sure that the attacker's right forearm is inside the defender's right forearm and that the attacker's upper arm is tucked in between the defender's upper arm and the right side of the defender's body. Once the arm lock is set, the defender can let go with his left hand. The defender will then press the back of the attacker's wrist toward himself to secure compliance.

Two-Finger Press Proper Rear Arm Lock
(*Yubi Shimi Waza*)

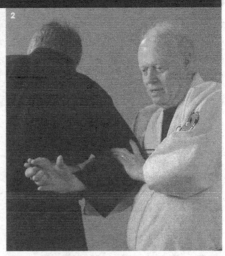

Once the defender has the attacker's arm behind the attacker, ...

... the defender should start to bend two of the attacker's fingers back, turning the attacker's wrist straight at the same time.

The defender will bend the grabbed two fingers of the attacker back to finish turning the attacker's hand palm-down, establishing control of the attacker.

Note: This variation is a more effective arm lock for a person with small hands.

Arm Lock
(*Ude Guruma*) 779—for a Trapping Handshake

The attacker (left) grips the defender's right hand hard to trap it so the defender can't use it.

The defender's left hand forms a *gingitzu*, which is a fist with a slightly protruding middle-finger knuckle. A gingitzu is used to strike relatively soft tissue areas.

The defender strikes down across the back of the attacker's hand ...

... and hits the attacker's radial or digital nerve. This is done to release the grip of the handshake or act as a distraction.

The defender's right hand keeps hold of either the attacker's right hand or thumb (if the attacker tries to retract his hand).

The defender's left hand grabs onto the attacker's right elbow.

The defender pulls the attacker's elbow forward as the defender pushes the attacker's right hand toward his right side by applying pressure to the base of the opponent's thumb.

The defender starts to bring the attacker's hand up behind the attacker's back.

Continued ➡

The defender raises the attacker's hand up his back and hooks the attacker's elbow in between the defender's right upper arm and the defender's chest.

The defender's left hand comes up under the attacker's right hand.

The defender's right hand lets go of the attacker's thumb and slides to get down to the back of the attacker's right hand ...

... and sets up a wrist-press arm lock. The defender's left hand holds the attacker's right arm in place ...

... until the wrist press is secured. Then the defender can let go with his left hand.

Shoulder Locks

Shoulder-Lock Wrist-Press Submission (*Ude Makikomi Shimi Waza*) 46

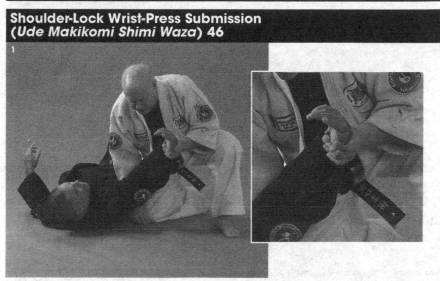

This submission is performed after the defender (top) has thrown the attacker and the attacker is down. The defender's right knee is next to the attacker. At this point, the defender should have a secure C-grip on the attacker's right wrist.

The defender leans against the attacker's chest. The defender's right arm goes under the attacker's right upper arm and over to "hook" the attacker's right arm, which is bent by the hooking motion.

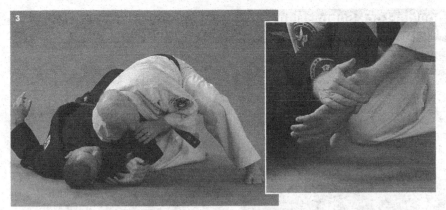

The defender's left hand forms a cup (*sara*) and hooks the top back part of the attacker's elbow.

Note: Your left leg will start to push up, which puts more weight on the right side of the attacker's chest just inside his shoulder joint.

With the defender's shoulder firmly pressing down on the front of the attacker's shoulder and the back of the attacker's hand firmly on the ground, the defender pulls the attacker's forearm toward himself at the attacker's wrist while the defender pushes away and down with his left hand at the attacker's elbow. The defender also applies a forward and downward motion with his torso.

This sets up a very effective wrist press with a very strong shoulder lock at the same time. The more the attacker's elbow is pushed forward, the more effective both joint submissions become. If executed quickly, this technique can dislocate the attacker's shoulder and break the attacker's wrist.

115

Shoulder-Lock Submission From Behind (*Senaka Shimi Waza*) 184—Attacker Is Sitting or Getting Up

As the attacker gets up, the defender approaches the attacker from behind.

The defender's left arm goes between the attacker's left upper arm and torso.

The defender's left arm comes up, raising the attacker's arm toward the attacker's head and unbalancing him.

The defender's left hand comes around to the right side of attacker's neck, at the base of his head, and quickly turns the attacker's head to the attacker's left before the attacker can resist.

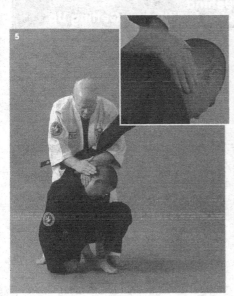

The defender's right hand presses down on the defender's left hand, thus securing the position of the attacker's head and turning the attacker farther to the left. The defender's right knee is in the attacker's back, serving as a fulcrum to rotate the attacker's body to the defender's left on his y-axis.

The defender moves his left foot back while maintaining pressure on the attacker's neck and rotating counterclockwise to his own left ...

... to bring the attacker down to the ground.

The defender maintains the pin by keeping the attacker's left arm extended upward and the attacker's head turned down and to the left. In essence, the attacker's shoulder joint is being compressed toward the neck and head.

117

Shoulder-Lock Submission From Behind
(*Senaka Shimi Waza*) 184—Attacker Is Sitting or Getting Up

In this variation, the defender's left hand goes in front of attacker's left arm ...

... and hooks the attacker's arm, trapping it.

The defender's left hand travels as far up the attacker's back as possible and ideally rests on the attacker's shoulder. The defender starts to set up a shoulder lock, which also begins to off-balance the attacker.

The defender rests his right hand on the top of his left hand and applies more pressure to the shoulder lock. The defender's right knee is on the attacker's back to provide a pivot point for rotating the attacker to the defender's left.

The defender applies more pressure to the shoulder lock as the defender pivots his left foot back in a counterclockwise circle to bring the attacker down to the ground.

The defender then applies downward pressure with his hands, as the defender leans forward, thus increasing pressure on the attacker's shoulder from the attacker's extended arm, which is still trapped and rotated forward. The defender may rest his right knee on the attacker's kidney for added effect and to enhance the shoulder lock, as well.

Shoulder-Lock Pin
(*Senaka Shimi Waza*) 741—for After a Throw (Such as a Body Winding Throw—*Karada Makikomi*)

The defender (top) has thrown the attacker and the defender's right arm is around the attacker's head so that the defender can set up a head lock. The attacker's right arm is bent so that the defender can't set a figure-4 armbar on the attacker's right arm. The defender makes sure that his armpit is on the attacker's neck and under the attacker's chin, thus blocking the attacker's chin, so the defender can set an effective head lock on the attacker.

Continued ▶

The defender grabs the attacker's right forearm with his left hand.

The defender's right hand grabs the attacker's right forearm at the attacker's wrist.

The defender holds onto the attacker's wrist as the defender's left hand moves up to the attacker's elbow from behind and pushes it up toward the attacker's head.

Note: Your chest is against the attacker's upper arm, and the back of the attacker's hand is bent against the ground.

The defender places his own left hand on top of his own right hand to provide additional support at the attacker's wrist. The defender's body continues to apply pressure to the back of the attacker's upper arm.

The defender rolls forward toward the attacker's head, thus applying more pressure on the back of the attacker's arm and downward pressure on the attacker's bent wrist and the attacker's shoulder. The defender' right hand maintains the hook on the attacker's right forearm as the defender's left hand pulls the attacker's bent forearm toward the defender, bending the attacker's wrist more. In addition, it sets a shoulder-lock pin and secures the head lock. It does seem like there's a lot going on here, but the defender now has a head lock, shoulder lock and wrist press—all in a neat little row.

As an alternative, the defender may want to hook his own left hand over his own right forearm and pull to set the head-lock, shoulder-lock or wrist-press submission here.

Shoulder-Lock Pin
(*Gyaku Ude Guruma*) 829—Submission After a Throw

The attacker is on his left side or stomach, and the defender is holding the attacker's right arm at the attacker's shoulder with the defender's right hand.

The defender's left arm slips in under the attacker's forearm. The defender's right arm pulls the attacker's sleeve, midway between his elbow and shoulder, toward the defender. Gripping the attacker at a point between his elbow and shoulder, the defender pulls the attacker's sleeve in a clockwise direction (to the defender's right). This puts the attacker farther on his left side toward his stomach.

The defender continues to pull the attacker's arm toward the defender as the defender's bent left arm sets an arm lock on the attacker's right arm. At the same time, the defender's left hand reaches toward the attacker's right shoulder. Notice that the attacker's left arm is not under his body but is visible.

Once the defender's left hand reaches the attacker's shoulder, the defender's right hand lets go of the attacker's sleeve and rests on top of the defender's left hand so the defender can push down with it.

If the attacker's left arm is trapped under his own body, that's OK at this point. The defender goes down onto his left knee so that he can apply his full body weight to the back of the attacker's right shoulder. At this point, the defender has set a figure-4 shoulder lock. However, for the defender to protect himself, he needs to pursue the shoulder lock further, either dislocating the attacker's shoulder by raising the arm lock up with the defender's left forearm as the defender presses down on the attacker's shoulder or the defender can add the following two steps.

The defender needs to give two clear verbal commands at this point: 1) "Turn your head the other way." If the attacker does NOT comply, the defender will exert a bit more pressure on the attacker's right shoulder. The defender then eases up on the shoulder pressure for a moment as the defender repeats the command. 2) Once the attacker has complied, the defender then gives the second command: "Get your arm out from under you." Again, the defender may use some compliance pressure to secure compliance. (Although his trapped arm creates a higher level of discomfort for him, the defender's safety dictates that the defender needs to see what may be in the attacker's hand—perhaps a weapon that could be used against the defender.)

Once the attacker has complied with the defender's two requests, the attacker will feel more comfortable—momentarily—until the defender exerts more downward pressure on the attacker's right shoulder. (This is now easier to do because the attacker's head is turned away, naturally lowering his shoulder a bit to bring it down to the ground.) The defender's left forearm also moves upward, thus raising the attacker's locked arm and effectively setting the figure-4 shoulder lock on the attacker.

Shoulder-Lock Pin
(Ude Gatame) 847

The attacker is on his back, and the defender is at the attacker's right side after a basic hand throw *(te nage/kote gaeshi)*.

The defender goes down onto his right knee, blocking the attacker's head with his left shin.

The defender rolls back, rotating to the right on the defender's y-axis. The defender's left foot/shin guides the attacker in the same direction (to land facedown) by applying pressure to the back of the attacker's neck at the base of the attacker's skull.

The defender continues the rotation, ...

... bringing the defender and the attacker over into the following position. During the entire rotation, the defender keeps hold of the attacker's wrist.

The defender hooks his left foot over the back of the prone attacker's neck. By being in this position, with the defender's right foot up, the defender can control the amount of pressure applied to the back of the attacker's neck by shifting the defender's body weight.

Note: If you place too much weight on the attacker's neck, serious injuries can occur.

In order to set a shoulder-lock pin, the defender will need to carefully sit on the attacker's shoulder (which may put weight on the back of the attacker's neck), so he must be careful.

The defender sets the wrist press as shown. (See close-up.) The defender also lifts the attacker's locked (joint-dampened) arm up toward the defender to execute the shoulder-lock pin. The defender hooks his hands so that the *ki* can be directed upward and inward toward the attacker's shoulder.

Shoulder-Lock Rear Takedown (*Ude Guruma Ushiro*) 875—for Handshake

The defender's left hand slaps the back of the attacker's hand as a distraction.

The defender keeps hold of the attacker's hand as the defender ...

... steps toward the attacker with his left foot, turning slightly to the defender's right so that the defender's left forearm is parallel to and in full contact with the attacker's right forearm.

The defender continues to turn clockwise as the defender brings the attacker's arm up. The defender maintains full forearm contact as he turns. The defender stays as close to the attacker as possible.

The defender continues the clockwise rotation as the defender establishes full contact between his own arm and the attacker's upper arm. This contact ensures that the defender is as close as possible to the attacker. This close full-contact rotation also makes it very difficult for the attacker to turn out of the hold being set up by the defender.

As the defender finishes the completed turn, the defender is now facing the opposite direction of the attacker. The shoulder lock will now be set for execution.

The defender pulls down on the attacker's right wrist with both the defender's hands (C-grip), off-balancing the attacker, dislocating and separating the attacker's shoulder if he resists, ...

Continued

... and throwing him backward.

Caution: If executed at normal speed on the street, this technique may cause severe and permanent shoulder damage.

In practice, the defender should pull down on the attacker's wrist only as fast as the defender can safely fall. The defender should NOT get ahead of the attacker in practice.

Shoulder-Lock Comealong for a Handshake (*Ude Guruma Shimi Waza*)

The defender proceeds through the same steps as the previous technique, a shoulder-lock rear takedown, until the shoulder lock is set.

The defender places his left hand on the back of the attacker's upper arm just above his elbow as the defender continues to turn clockwise. The defender ends up facing the same direction as the attacker. The defender keeps hold of the attacker's right hand by maintaining the original handshake grip with the defender's right hand. The defender should also make sure that his left forearm (near the defender's elbow) is against the back of the attacker's neck. This sets a base and prevents the attacker from turning to his right and into the defender.

The defender uses his left hand to pull the attacker's arm back, thus off-balancing the attacker. To establish better control of the attacker, the defender uses the original handshake to turn the attacker's hand to the defender's right. (Whether the attacker's right wrist is bent is irrelevant—although a bent wrist is better for the defender's control.) By slightly twisting the attacker's wrist, the defender creates enough pain to move the attacker in any direction or uses the trapped attacker as a shield against other attackers.

Caution: Be very careful turning the attacker's wrist when the attacker's arm is in this locked position. Just a little turning will cause a great deal of pain. Too much turning will break his wrist. If you break the attacker's wrist, you will lose all control of the attacker.

Shoulder-Lock Rear Throw
(*Ude Guruma Ushiro*)—for an Overhead Club Attack

The attacker is swinging down at the defender with an overhead club. The defender brings both his own arms up, right over left, crossing them at midforearm, with his own hands closed into fists.

The defender steps toward the attacker with his left foot as he aggressively cross-blocks the attacker's forearm with both his forearms. The defender's block should then immediately deflect the force of the attack slightly to the defender's right. The defender should form fists to establish more power and reduce the chance of injuring his hands and fingers.

The defender's right forearm continues to block the attacker's arm as the defender's left hand securely grabs the attacker's arm at the attacker's wrist, thus preventing the attacker from moving or bending his own hand. The close-up shows the defender's grip on the attacker's wrist. Surprisingly, the pointed index finger allows for an extension of *ki* that will help maintain the defender's grip and the steps that follow.

The defender's right hand strikes the attacker's elbow with a knife-edge strike to bend the attacker's arm.

Continued ➤

Immediately after bending the arm, the defender's left hand bends the attacker's right hand palm down with the attacker's fingers pointing toward the attacker's body.

The defender's right arm then goes under the attacker's upper arm and ...

... hooks onto the top (backside) of the attacker's bent right hand.

The defender starts to push forward and downward in a circular motion away from the defender, with the defender's right hand (which is on top of the attacker's right hand at a right angle) pointed in the direction the defender wants the attacker to fall—backward.

Shoulder-Lock Rear Takedown
(*Ude Guruma Ushiro*)—for a High Backhand Knife Swipe

The attacker (left) is ready to attack.

The defender leans back or steps back to get out of the way of the forward knife swipe by the attacker.

Once the knife swipe passes, the defender steps in quickly. The defender brings both his own forearms up to aggressively block the backhand swipe by the attacker. (The defender should make sure both his hands are in fists for extra protection.) The defender's left forearm should block the attacker's upper arm, and the defender's right forearm should block the attacker's forearm just below the attacker's elbow. (This type of block will keep the defender's right forearm as far away from the knife blade as possible. This is especially important if the attacker has bent his wrist so that the knife blade is against the backside of the attacker's forearm with the sharp edge outward.)

The defender immediately pushes the attacker's right forearm up and back until it bends at the attacker's elbow. The defender's left hand reaches over the attacker's upper arm and ...

... hooks onto the defender's right forearm, thus setting up a figure 4 lock.

Note: Your right forearm should be resting on the attacker's forearm.

Hooking onto the attacker's right forearm with the defender's right hand will actually prevent the attacker's elbow from bending as much and leverage will be more difficult to apply by the defender.

The defender should now have a well-set figure-4 lock. The defender simply continues the downward motion to the attacker's rear to execute the technique.

Shoulder-Lock Rear Throw
(*Ude Guruma Ushiro*)—for a Right Hit

The attacker (left) has initiated a straight punch to the defender's face with his right fist. The defender is in a "ready position" (*tachi waza*) and is prepared to block or deflect the hit.

The defender blocks the attacker's hit outward with his left forearm.

The defender's right forearm comes in under the attacker's right upper arm all the way to the defender's elbow, if possible. The defender's left forearm collapses somewhat by bending at the elbow so the defender can push his own forearm toward the attacker and back. The defender's right forearm is "thumbs up," which means the back of his arm is resting against the radial edge of the defender's arm. The defender's right foot steps in at the same time. The defender continues to block with his left forearm.

The defender pulls his right forearm toward himself as he pushes the attacker's right forearm with his left forearm. This will cause the attacker's upper arm to rotate counterclockwise, locking his shoulder joint (joint dampening) and off-balancing the attacker toward the attacker's rear.

The defender continues this motion ...

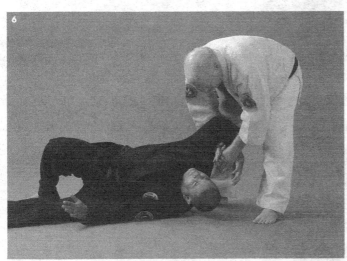

... so that the attacker falls backward. At no time does the defender grab the attacker's arm with either hand. To do so would have signaled what the defender was going to do.

Note: This is an incredibly fast rear shoulder lock because it gives absolutely no warning until the rear shoulder lock is well under way. Resistance is completely counterproductive for the attacker once the shoulder lock is set to be executed.

Shoulder-Lock Rear Takedown
(*Ude Guruma Ushiro*)—Forward Elbow Lift for a Side Muscle Grab

The attacker grabs the defender's left upper sleeve or arm and attempts to push the defender forward. This attack is sometimes called a "bum's rush" or side muscle grab. (It's a technique usually used by people who are not properly trained to move people.)

The forward elbow lift is shown as a variation of a rear shoulder lock for two reasons: First, it is a figure-4 lock. Second, it rotates the y-axis of the attacker's upper arm in the same direction as the other shoulder locks, thus dampening the shoulder joint (parent joint) and causing the attacker to fall backward. The same action is being created except that the counterclockwise rotation is moving up from the elbow rather than downward, which is a 180-degree difference.

The defender moves in the direction the attacker wants the defender to move for one to two steps. The defender then starts to turn toward the attacker as the defender raises his left arm. The reason that the defender takes one to two steps is to distract the attacker and to create some momentum (*ki* movement) on the attacker's part, which makes it easier to complete the rest of the technique.

The defender slightly steps in to the attacker as the defender rotates his entire arm counterclockwise. This movement will negate the forward pressure the attacker has on the defender's upper arm. The defender has created crotch space.

The defender continues the counterclockwise circle as the top of the defender's left forearm comes in contact with the backside of the attacker's elbow. The defender should make sure that his palm is facing down and that he makes contact with the backside of the attacker's elbow about two-thirds of the way down the defender's forearm, toward the defender's wrist. This will give the defender maximum leverage and torque as he ...

... rotates the attacker's bent arm forward and up at the attacker's elbow, off-balancing the attacker. Also note that the attacker's right wrist and forearm are trapped in the defender's armpit.

The defender now has a very effective comealong set. If the attacker resists, compliance can be re-established by raising his elbow forward and up slightly in the same circular motion used to set up the figure-4 lock. The comealong can be easily maintained with one hand if the defender keeps both his palms facing down and the attacker's elbow centered on the lower third of the defender's forearm.

Continued ➡

If the defender senses too much resistance or the defender wants to execute a shoulder-lock rear throw, the defender's right hand (palm-up) grabs his own left hand (palm-down) ...

... and raises the attacker's elbow upward, in the same direction as the circular movement to set the figure-4 lock, as the defender pivots his left foot back. In practice, the defender should only start to raise the attacker's elbow up and only start to pivot his left foot back.

Caution: Serious injury to the attacker most likely will occur if you attempt to complete this shoulder-lock rear throw, even in practice. There are some techniques in *budoshin jujitsu* that can not be completed in practice because the injury risk is just too high.

Shoulder-Lock Takedown (*Senaka Gatame*) 877—for a Rear Shoulder Grab to the Defender's Right Shoulder

The attacker's right hand grabs the defender's right shoulder from behind.

The defender turns clockwise to the defender's right, raising his right arm up as he turns to face the same direction as the attacker.

The defender's right arm continues circling, trapping the attacker's right arm.

The defender's left hand rests on the attacker's right shoulder.

Continued ➡

The defender's right hand, palm-down, hooks onto his own left forearm. It almost looks like a figure-4 armbar except that the attacker's elbow (backside) is facing up.

The defender rolls the attacker's shoulder forward ...

... as the defender brings the attacker down ...

... to the ground.

The defender then brings his left foot over the attacker's right shoulder as he ...

... sits down on the attacker's right shoulder. Even though it feels like the figure-4 has been lost, the defender should maintain the hold as best as possible.

Note: The position of your left knee is down. This adds additional pressure to the top of the attacker's shoulder, keeping the attacker in place.

The defender brings his right leg into a somewhat cross-legged position. This will be a more comfortable position for the defender. The defender can keep the attacker's arm in place (along the defender's right hip joint) by simply applying downward pressure with the defender's right forearm.

Not shown: If the defender senses any resistance by the attacker, the defender can simply roll back onto his own back. He brings his own right arm over to his own left hip joint and set a figure-4 armbar.

Leg and Hip Locks

Beginner's Figure-4 Leg Lock (*Ashi No Hiki Shimi Waza*) 196

The defender has completed a leg-lift rear throw (*ashi ushiro nage*) and rotated the attacker onto his stomach by turning the attacker's right ankle clockwise. The defender grabs the attacker's left foot ...

... and places it on the back of the attacker's right knee joint.

The defender then bends the attacker's right leg ...

... over the attacker's left foot, trapping it.

The defender kneels down on the attacker's lower leg and leans forward to secure the submission.

Proper Figure-4 Leg Lock
(*Ashi No Hiki Shimi Waza*) 196

Once a student gets to sixth *kyu* (usually a new student's first belt promotion), the student should learn this more advanced and street-safer version of the figure-4 leg lock. The defender grabs the attacker's right foot with both his hands and lifts the attacker's foot off the ground.

The defender places his right foot over and to the left side of the attacker's right kneecap, with the defender's foot (toes) pointing toward the attacker's crotch. This helps the defender line up his leg so he can drop down onto his right leg and set up a figure-4 lock.

Once the defender's right foot is on the ground, the defender starts to slowly squat down by bending his own right leg.

The defender kneels down on his right knee. The defender's right lower leg should be at a right angle to the attacker's right leg (for maximum comfort of both parties and maximum effectiveness of the figure-4 lock).

The defender moves his left foot up next to the attacker's left hip so that the defender is in a balanced position. Notice that the attacker's right foot points to the right toward the defender's right side. Pointing the attacker's right foot at the defender's right side rather than the defender's left negates the strength and leverage of the attacker's right foot. This is because most of the defender's weight is in front of the attacker's ankle rather than behind it.

Continued ▶

The defender leans forward very slowly to hyperextend the attacker's right knee joint, giving the attacker a chance to give up or tap out.

Caution: Don't stand up to release the hold. The only safe way out of this figure-4 leg lock is for the defender to roll back and to his right, ...

... rolling out of the lock ...

... and rolling away before he gets up in a ready position. (If the defender attempts to get out by standing up, he can easily lose his balance and break both his and the attacker's right leg when the defender falls back down.)

Striking Technique With Figure-4 Leg-Lock Submission (*Atemi Waza Ashi Gatame*) 220—for Shoulder Grab and Pull From Behind With Right Hand

The attacker grabs the defender's right shoulder from behind.

As the attacker pulls the defender around, the defender's right backhand snaps back and ...

... strikes the side base of the attacker's ribs or stomach.

The defender continues the clockwise turn to the attacker's right. The defender then goes back down onto his right knee, facing the attacker.

The defender strikes at the attacker's groin or lower abdomen with his right fist.

The defender grabs the attacker's right leg as he steps forward with his left foot and drops down onto his right knee.

The defender uses his left hand to lift the attacker's leg at the ankle ...

... and pushes against the attacker's knee joint with his right forearm to lock the attacker's knee joint, causing the attacker to fall back.

Once the attacker is on the ground, the defender can go to any one of the following finishing holds, locks or submissions on pages 152 to 155.

Figure-4 Hip Brace
(*Koshi Gatame*) 872—Figure-4 Knee-Brace Submission for a Front Kick

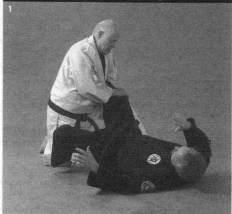

The attacker is on the ground, and the defender is holding onto the attacker's right leg.

Caution: When practicing this submission, you need to set it up and execute it very slowly to avoid injuring your practice partner.

Start to set up a figure-4 hip brace (*koshi gatame*). The defender rotates his own left forearm clockwise so that ...

... it can go to the inside and under the attacker's right foreleg. The defender's right hand is removed from the attacker's kneecap in the close-up only because it presents a clearer view of the defender's left forearm and hand.

The defender brings his left arm under the attacker's right leg as the defender's right hand starts to turn the attacker's leg to the left ...

... and in toward the defender's body.

This helps turn the attacker's body onto his left side.

The defender stands up as he hooks the attacker's right foot against the defender's left side at his hip (x-axis).

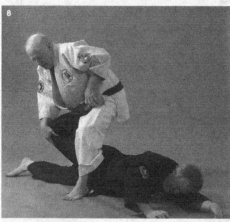

The defender steps over the attacker with his left foot.

Caution: Proceed very slowly from this point onward to avoid seriously injuring the attacker's hip joint.

Note: Your left calf is against the attacker's body at the attacker's hip so he can't turn onto his stomach.

The defender drops down (very slowly in practice) onto the ground with his own right knee. At this point, the y-axis of the defender's body and the y-axis of the attacker's leg are perpendicular to each other. Also, the y-axis of the defender's body and left leg are both perpendicular to the y-axis of the attacker's body. (Two right angles equal a figure-4 lock.)

The defender rotates clockwise to his right on his y-axis (meaning the defender turns his body to his right) to execute the submission.

Figure-4 Hip Brace/Lock

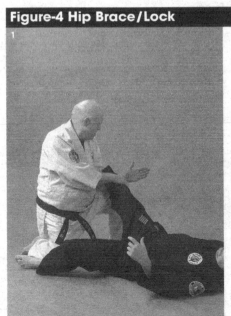

The defender can use the following technique against a kick (starting with the next picture), or the attacker can be on the ground with the defender's left arm hooked onto the attacker's right leg, like it was in the previous technique.

The defender (left) and the attacker are in a ready position (*tachi waza*).

Continued ➡

The defender deflects the force of the attacker's kick to the defender's left. The defender has a closed fist for a stronger block and to protect his fingers from injury from the kick.

The defender deflects the kick upward so he can trap the attacker's leg with his left forearm.

The defender starts to turn the attacker's leg to the defender's right as the defender steps in slightly to maintain his balance.

As the attacker's leg is turned clockwise, the attacker loses his balance and falls to the ground.

It may be necessary for the defender's right hand to clamp onto his own left hand to complete the throw.

The defender's left forearm moves toward the base of the attacker's calf to trap his ankle. The defender's right hand pushes down on the attacker's knee joint to keep the attacker off-balanced.

The attacker's right leg is lifted up so that ...

... the defender can step over the attacker with his left leg.

Caution: You must proceed very slowly from this point onward. Once your foot is on the ground, you should turn clockwise to your right very slowly.

Pins and Chokes

Cross-Block Reverse Pin (*Juji Ukemi*) 84—for Choke on the Ground

The attacker is attempting to choke the defender on the ground. The first thing the defender does is bend his right leg, keeping his right foot on the ground and sliding it up as close as possible to the bottom of his butt for maximum push.

The defender's right hand grabs high on the attacker's right collar. The defender's left hand grabs onto the attacker's right sleeve, slightly above the attacker's elbow.

The defender pulls the attacker's left lapel with his right hand and pushes against the attacker's right lapel with his left hand to off-balance the attacker toward the defender's right.

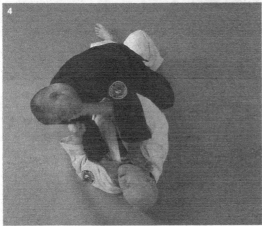

The defender switches the direction of the push-pull motion from the defender's right to his left as the defender pushes off with his right leg (to help get the attacker off the defender's body) as the defender's body rotates on its y-axis, turning to the defender's left.

The defender rolls on top of the attacker so that their y-axes are parallel to each other. This is not a safe position to remain in.

Continued ➤

The defender moves up on the attacker's body and starts to move in a perpendicular position.

The defender moves across the attacker's torso to get his y-axis perpendicular to the attacker's y-axis as the defender starts to set a reverse pin by moving the defender's left forearm under the attacker's head to set a reverse head lock. It's important for the defender to have his armpit under the attacker's chin because it restricts the attacker's movement once the reverse pin is set and prevents him from biting the defender.

The defender sets the reverse pin/ head lock and starts to rotate or roll back over the attacker's face.

The defender slowly rolls up the attacker's face, maintaining a reverse choke until he taps out.

Caution: Doing this quickly may cause extremely serious neck or spinal-cord injuries, especially if the attacker tries to escape.

Reverse-Choke Pin With Figure-4 Reverse Armbar (*Ude Guruma*)

As an alternative to the previous submission, the defender can set the reverse choke as shown or set a figure-4 reverse armbar by bringing the attacker's arm up over the defender's left thigh ...

... and pushing it down with his right hand as the defender leans back slightly.

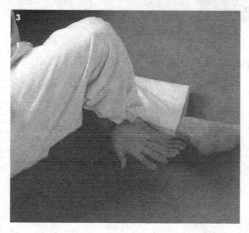

Another variation—especially if the attacker has bent his arm so that an armbar can no longer be set—is for the defender to hook his right foot as high as possible under his left calf to try to set up a shoulder lock.

Caution for Vascular/Carotid Neck Restraints
(*Kubi Shimi Waza*) 873—Three Variations of This Submission

EXTREME CAUTION:

1. To reduce the chance of serious and potentially permanent injury, this submission should be practiced from a sitting position until the practitioner has mastered it.

2. The defender makes sure that the back of the attacker's head and the first several vertebrae are against the defender's upper body during the entire submission to help avoid spinal injury.

3. The attacker should not resist or try to escape this hold in any form or manner because it could cause serious and potentially permanent injury to the attacker.

4. The defender should apply pressure slowly and release immediately when the training partner submits.

The three variations of this technique will go from most effective to least effective. The least effective variation is the one most commonly taught and is often incorrectly called a "police chokehold."

If your training attacker becomes unconscious or nonresponsive at any time during the execution of this technique, you should **IMMEDIATELY RELEASE THE HOLD** and secure medical assistance immediately by calling or having someone else **CALL 911 IMMEDIATELY!**

Vascular/Carotid Neck Restraint No. 1 (*Kubi Shimi Waza*)

Note: *This is the fastest and most effective of the three restraints presented. It is also the easiest to apply. It relies on attacking the nervous and vascular systems by cutting off the blood supply at the carotid arteries and applying pressure to various nerve centers along each side of the neck.*

Caution: *Apply pressure slowly and release immediately when the training partner submits. Follow all safety rules given at the beginning of this vascular-restraint segment.*

The defender's right arm goes around the attacker's neck ...

... from right to left.

Important: For safety reasons, make sure that the attacker is sitting on the ground and that you are kneeling behind the attacker, supporting the attacker's upper vertebrae.

The defender brings his arm around enough so that he can bend it, ideally at the front of the attacker's neck.

Note: This is a vascular neck restraint, which means it cuts off the blood supply to the brain and puts pressure on nerve centers. It doesn't cut off the air supply, so it's not a choke and doesn't require pressure against the front of the neck.

The defender's right hand rests on his left chest or preferably grabs his left lapel as high as possible on the his upper left arm.

The defender hooks at his right elbow only if he can't hook any higher.

Note: There is an ongoing debate on whether hooking onto your lapel is more effective than hooking onto your forearm. If you hook onto your lapel, a faster vascular restraint will result. However, its weakness is that there is no physical connection between your right and left arms. If you hook onto your forearm, it may give you a more secure hold, but the vascular restraint suffers because you squeeze rather than allow gravity to do the work. Practice and opportunity will determine which approach you come to prefer.

Continued ▶

The defender's left hand comes up and rests on the top backside of the attacker's head. Locking this up will apply pressure ONLY to both sides of the attacker's neck.

Caution: Make sure that the back of the attacker's head and the first several vertebrae are against your upper body to help avoid spinal injury.

The defender straightens his back SLOWLY. Then the defender will pull up SLOWLY and lean back SLOWLY to execute the submission. This is a relatively safe submission if the attacker doesn't resist.

Caution: Apply pressure slowly and release immediately when your training partner submits.

This submission will put a person "out" almost immediately if executed quickly and in two to five seconds if executed "slowly."

Not shown: In practice, if the attacker simulates resistance or attempts to push back against you, your easiest and safest counter is to roll back onto your back as you scissor (*hasami*) the attacker from behind or hook both of your feet inside the attacker's thighs, thereby splaying the attacker's body and extremities. You should practice this slowly and carefully.

Vascular/Carotid Neck Restraint No. 2
(Kubi Shimi Waza)

Note: *This is a compromise technique that relies mainly on vascular pressure, although some choking may also occur. Although still very effective, the attacker may also be choked during the restraining process.*

Caution: *Apply pressure slowly and release immediately when your training partner submits. Follow all safety rules given at the beginning of the vascular-restraint segment.*

The defender's right arm goes around the attacker's neck from right to left.

The defender brings his arm around enough so that he can bend it—ideally at the front of the attacker's neck.

Vascular/Carotid Neck Restraint No. 3
(*Kubi Shimi Waza*)—Rear Choke or Police Chokehold

Note: *Although this is supposed to be a vascular/carotid neck restraint, it is more of a choke. This compromise technique relies on vascular pressure and choking. Its dependency on strength makes it the most "heavy-handed" approach in the restraining process.*

The defender's right arm goes around the attacker's neck from right to left, with the defender's forearm in front and his right hand clamping onto his left upper arm. This essentially sets a head lock from behind and usually results in the defender's right upper arm actually choking the assailant rather than acting as a vascular/carotid restraint. The defender's left hand comes up and rests on the top backside of the attacker's head. Locking this up will apply pressure MAINLY to the front and left sides of attacker's neck. This hold creates the worst chin-to-elbow alignment.

Important: Make sure that the back of the attacker's head and the first several vertebrae are against the front of your upper body. You MUST support these upper vertebrae against your body during the entire submission process to help avoid spinal Injury.

The defender leans forward with his upper body, thus applying downward pressure at the front of the attacker's neck. This will also increase pressure on the sides of the attacker's neck.

Caution: Apply pressure slowly and release immediately when your training partner submits.

This submission will put a person "out" in one to 10 seconds, depending on where the pressure is applied to the attacker's neck.

Miscellaneous Techniques

Side Wrist Throw
(*Yoko Te Maki*) 876—for Resistance to the Basic Hand Throw

The defender (right) has set up a hand throw and is ready to execute it. However, the attacker resists (or the defender senses resistance to the original hand throw).

If the defender's right hand is also holding onto the attacker's bent right hand, the defender's right hand lets go of the attacker's right hand—the hand-throw setup. The defender's right hand goes under the attacker's forearm.

The defender's right hand then hooks onto the backside of the attacker's right hand, which is still bent.

Once the defender's right hand has a firm hook on the bent attacker's hand, the defender's left hand lets go of the hand-throw set and hooks onto the topside of the attacker's hand.

Continued ➤

The defender now rotates the attacker's hand outward (supination) and downward ...

... along the y-axis of the attacker's arm ...

... to bring the resistant attacker to the ground.

Caution: While practicing, you should do this very slowly to avoid breaking your attacker's wrist.

Little Finger Figure-4 Brace
(*Yubi Shimi Waza*) 878—for a Rear Waist Grab

Note: *Although this technique has great but subtle street applications, it has a greater value in teaching students how to maneuver a person using pain compliance. It is very difficult to break the little finger using this figure-4 brace, but if the defender can set this up properly, it's amazing how fast the attacker will move to avoid pain.*

The attacker wraps his arms around the defender's waist from behind.

The defender breaks the grip of the attacker's waist grab by any nerve or distraction technique. The defender's right hand brings the attacker's right hand down from the defender's waist to his side.

Continued ➤

The defender turns to his right, keeping the attacker's hand in front of the defender with the back of the attacker's hand toward the defender.

The defender keeps a firm grip on the attacker's wrist to keep his hand from turning and brings his own left hand up. The defender's left thumb slips under the attacker's right little finger between the little finger's nail and the first child joint—just above the first child joint. The defender's middle finger rests on top of the attacker's little finger between the second (child) joint and the little finger's knuckle (parent joint of the finger)—just above the knuckle on the little finger. This sets up a figure-4 lock. (Use the No. 4 concept if you don't believe me.)

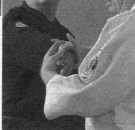

Once the defender gets the figure-4 lock set, the defender can start to control the direction and movement of the attacker. Notice that with a bit of downward pressure from the defender's middle finger and a bit of upward pressure from the defender's thumb (base), the defender can cause the attacker to start going down. This is identical to the figure-4 armbar—presented earlier in this book—in which the defender's right hand presses down slightly on the attacker's shoulder as the defender's other forearm pushes up slightly under the attacker's elbow. It is EXTREMELY important for the defender to keep both his fingers straight. The defender's hand and wrist movement can then control the direction of the pressure with ease.

The attacker moves down even more.

Continued ➡

The attacker is down. Once set, this is a totally effortless technique on the defender's part.

To cause the attacker to go up, the defender turns his own hand counterclockwise so his hand is facing up somewhat and applies pressure to the little finger, as described previously.

Play around with this figure-4 lock to see how many different directions and positions the attacker can be placed in.

Elbow-Lock Winding Throw (*Hiji Makikomi*) 879—for Double Hit or Wrist Grab From the Front

This throw may not look like a figure-4 lock, but it's an inherent part of setting up the throw.

As the attacker (left) swings with his right and left fists, the defender uses his left forearm to block the attacker's right arm.

At the same time, the defender's right forearm blocks the attacker's left fist out to the defender's right. The defender should step in with his right foot when he blocks using his right arm.

The defender slides both his forearms down each of the attacker's forearms to the attacker's wrists. The defender then grabs each of the attacker's wrists with a loose C-grip as the defender brings the attacker's left arm down in a clockwise circle ...

... and up under the attacker's right elbow, making sure that the elbows on both his arms are facing up. As an alternative, the defender may opt to bring the attacker's left arm up under the attacker's right armpit and still lock the attacker's right elbow.

The defender brings the attacker's right arm down (with the attacker's right elbow braced against the attacker's left arm from on top) in a downward circle to the defender's left as the defender pivots his left foot back ...

... to throw the attacker ...

... to the ground. In practice, the defender should let go of the attacker's left arm as the attacker is being thrown so the attacker can break his fall.

CONCLUDING REMARKS

As a concept, figure-4 locks are a concept that revolve around a spatial alignment of your and your opponent's extremities. Regardless of the situation or opponent, there are standard ways to get into, set up and execute figure-4 locks. Some are more effective than others. Some are easier to set up than others. Some will result in a faster submission or a serious and potentially permanent injury.

Figure-4 locks are extremely effective, both as pain-compliance techniques and as submission or physically disabling techniques. With practice, you will develop the sensitivity needed not only to effectively execute figure-4 locks but also to feel exactly what you are doing to the attacker's body. This, in turn, will help you determine how much pain or discomfort you are creating before any serious injury occurs. What you do with the locks depends on the situation you are in. This flexibility is an asset for you.

Many years ago, one of my black-belt students very excitedly came to class and told me, "It worked. The jujitsu worked." I sat her down and asked what had happened because she was also concerned about being arrested. Apparently, some guy pulled a knife on her at a bus stop. She promptly reacted with a basic hand throw (*te nage*) that broke his wrist and ended the assault. She was afraid to go to the police. To make a long story short, we contacted the police, and the assailant was found at a local high school. A cast on his wrist narrowed down the possible suspects. He was arrested, tried and convicted of attempted assault with a deadly weapon.

Why am I bringing up this short tale at the end of this book? Because this particular student said an identical set of magic words that all my students (fortunately very few) have said after an attack: "It worked. The jujitsu worked."

Well, jujitsu is supposed to work. That's why it's been around for so long. That's why the samurai in Japan trained in it so extensively. Simply stated, it works! Admittedly, teaching methods have changed over the years to help students learn the art more effectively. Wally Jay's "small-circle theory" and Steve Heremaia's "10 concepts" are just two of the major teaching methodologies used to influence and improve traditional jujitsu.

Techniques from jujitsu and any other traditional martial art will work if they're executed properly. Of course, nothing works as neatly on the street as it does in the controlled environment of the dojo. However, if you've practiced your techniques over and over and over (*ad infinitum agnosium*) to the point at which you can execute techniques in a state of mushin during street-attack simulations, your chances of success on the street will be vastly improved.

In line with this, what is important for you to remember and understand from *Jujitsu Figure-4 Locks* is the characteristics of setting up and executing figure-4 locks. Once you get these concepts down (with lots of practice), you'll see their simplicity. Names will become irrelevant. You'll be amazed at how easy it will be for you to set them up in different situations. Once you get the concept etched into your mind, application is a bit of a no-brainer. You've achieved a state of mushin with respect to figure-4 locks. Also, keep in mind that it's the simple techniques that work best on the street because they are simple.

Sometimes, as we get older and hopefully wiser, we attempt to simplify the learning process for others. I now realize that no one can really remember "x" number of techniques or "all" the techniques that make up any system of any martial art. After all, perhaps in this context "all" is an infinite number. Maybe this is why learning concepts is just as valuable or more valuable than learning "x" number of techniques. Maybe what is important is learning the concepts and being able to apply them in many situations.

There's an old saying: "Give a man a fish and he can eat for a day. Teach a man how to fish and he can feed his family forever." Maybe teaching a man how to fish (or helping him learn a concept) is more important than simply giving him a fish (or teaching him a single technique).

After 42 years, I am still learning the art of jujitsu. Amazingly, after all this time, I am back to the basics. I am looking at the basic movements of jujitsu and basic movements within each technique of jujitsu, hoping to find more commonalities that will simplify the art for me, my students and you. I still keep going through the five-step process over and over again. The base keeps moving, expanding and growing. Maybe by moving toward "concept" techniques, I am trying to simplify the art—for others such as you as well as myself.

What will this do for the art of jujitsu? Good things, I hope.

Glossary for *Figure-4 Locks*

aikido
Aikido is a martial art derived directly from traditional *jujitsu*. The name combines three elements—*ai* = mind, *ki* = spirit, *do* = way—and emphasizes redirecting an attacker's energy flow (ki) in another direction. It places an extremely high value on nonviolence, inner calm, the avoidance of violence, and minimum injury to the attacker whenever possible.

ashi no hiki shimi waza*
Foot-lift rear throw and figure-4 leg lock. *Ashi* = foot/leg; *no* = a grammatical transitional possessive phrase; *shimi* = pain, choke or strangling; *waza* = technique.

ashi shimi waza*
Figure-4 leg lock. *Ashi* = foot/leg; *shimi* = pain, choke or strangling; *waza* = technique.

ashi shimi waza*
Leg lock. *Ashi* = foot/leg; *shimi* = pain, choke or strangling; *waza* = technique.

attacker
The attacker is the person who is attacking the defender. He is your training partner. When you switch roles and then attack your training partner, you become the attacker and your partner is the defender.

axial rotation
Axial rotation is the turning or twisting of the human body or an extremity (arm, leg, head, fingers, toes, hand, foot) along its length or y-axis.

axis (x, y, z)
The body has three axes.

1) The y-axis is the vertical axis that descends down from the center of your head to your feet and is perpendicular to the ground.

2) The x-axis is a straight line and parallel to the ground. (When you're in a standing position that extends out to the left and right of your body, it extends from the zero point of the y-axis.

3) The z-axis is identical to the x-axis except that it extends to your front and rear. It is also perpendicular to your x-axis at all times.

Also, it can be argued that all the joints on your extremities have their own x-y-z axis, which is what makes joint locks and figure-4 locks workable.

block (a hit or kick)
The purpose of a block is to stop a hit or kick from traveling in the direction it seeks to go. It ideally requires a counterforce at a right angle (90 degrees) to the direction of the momentum of the attack.

comealong
A hold placed on the attacker that allows you to use pain compliance to secure his cooperation. Comealongs, from the term "come along with me," are used to move a person from one place to another. The attacker has both his feet on the ground.

compliance
Compliance can mean any of the following:

1) You will do as I tell you or encourage you to do to avoid pain or discomfort.
2) Something you do to cooperate with or follow the directions of another person.
3) The actual verbal and/or physical action taken to secure cooperation.
4) The result of cooperation.

defender
The defender is the person executing a technique or *kata*.

deflect (a hit or kick)
The purpose of a deflection is to redirect the direction a hit or kick seeks to go rather than stop its momentum. The counterforce is executed at an angle significantly greater or less than a right angle (90 degrees) to the direction of the momentum of the attack. Deflections are used in order to use the attacker's *ki* (or energy flow) as part of your defensive technique.

extremity
Any body part that emanates from the skeletal structure of your torso (arm, leg, head, fingers, toes, hand, foot).

gyaku shimi waza*

Reverse shoulder-lock pin. *Gyaku* = reverse; *shimi* = pain, choke or strangling; *waza* = technique.

gyaku shioku gatame*

Reverse head lock. *Gyaku* = reverse, *shioku* = nerve, *gatame* = grapple.

gyaku ude guruma*

Reverse shoulder-lock pin. *Gyaku* = reverse, *ude* = arm, *guruma* (*kuruma*) = circular (wraparound).

gyaku waza makikomi*

Winding armbar. *Gyaku* = reverse, *waza* = technique, *makikomi* = winding throw.

hara

The *hara* is the center or balance point of the human body and can also be referred to as the *saiki tanden* or zero point in the x-y-z axes.

hiza tatake*

Figure-4 leg lock with ankle lock. *Hiza* = knee, *tatake* = attack.

humanoid joint

The humanoid joint is located at the sacrum. This is considered to be the root joint of the human body because off-balancing this joint makes all techniques in all martial arts possible. There is some argument that the humanoid joint is the atlas joint because it connects the top of the vertebrae and the base of the skull. As a result, the human body will go whichever direction the head goes. However, to effectively off-balance someone requires that the sacrum be affected in terms of destabilizing the y-axis (vertical axis).

joint (parent/child)

A joint is a point in the skeletal structure at which two or more bones connect to each other via ligaments, which limit or allow movement in various directions while providing support for that movement.

1) A child joint is any joint below a parent joint.

2) A parent joint connects an extremity to the torso. It is the top joint in a joint-chain hierarchy and is usually the closest one to the skull in humans.

joint (synovial)
Synovial joints are the most common joints in the human body. Their flexibility, direction and freedom of movement are determined by their design.

joint rotation (on axis)
This occurs when an extremity is turned (torqued) clockwise or counterclockwise along its length (or y-axis). Turning an extremity ultimately results in also turning the joints of the extremity until the ligaments reach their limit. Joint dampening occurs when the joint can no longer be turned, thus causing the joint to "lock" as joint resistance occurs.

joint chain
A joint chain is a series of joints that connect to each other. (e.g., shoulder joint to elbow joint to wrist joint to finger joints.)

joint-chain hierarchy
The joint-chain hierarchy begins with the parent joint, which is the highest joint in the chain's hierarchy, and ends with one or more child joints. (c.g., shoulder joint to elbow joint to wrist joint to finger joints).

joint dampening
Joint dampening represents the increased inability of a joint to move in a particular direction because the ligaments connecting the bones of the joint have reached their limit of movement.

joint resistance
Same as joint dampening, above.

judo
Judo is a sport (and also a self-defense system) that evolved from *jujitsu*. Judo founder Jigoro Kano created the art because he wanted to make jujitsu "safe" and improve jujitsu's bad reputation in Japan in the latter half of the 19th century. *Ju* = gentle, *do* = way.

juji ukemi*
Cross-block reverse pin. *Juji* = cross-block, *ukemi* = fall.

jujitsu

Jujitsu—ju = gentle, *jitsu* = art—is known as the gentle art of self-defense. The more modern arts of *aikido*, judo and some styles of karate directly evolved from traditional jujitsu. Traditional jujitsu is sometimes referred to as a "parent" art because many more "modern" martial arts have evolved from it. A major reason for this "breakup" was that the vast and complex makeup of jujitsu made it difficult to master because it covered so many areas of self-defense. For the samurai, jujitsu was the martial art of choice for survival on the battlefield.

karate

Karate (or *karate-do*) is a martial art that involves strikes and hits with the hand, elbow, foot or kneecap, depending on the style (*ryu*). *Kara* = empty, *te* = hand, *do* = way.

kata

Kata literally means "form." In *jujitsu*, a kata would be a single specific technique, such as a hip throw (*koshi nage*), hand throw (*te nage*) or a shoulder-lock rear takedown (*ude guruma ushiro*). The execution of kata in jujitsu require a training partner. In most styles of karate, a form is usually a series of blocking, maneuvering hitting and kicking techniques brought together to form a viable sequence of responses to a single attacker or multiple attackers. No training partner is used in a kata in karate.

kata practice

Kata practice is a term applicable to all martial arts in which certain techniques or moves are repeated over and over again, with the goal of achieving perfect execution of the kata from a state of *mushin*.

ki

Ki essentially translates into the spirit or energy within your body. The use and extension of your ki determines your success in anything you do.

ki alignment

In a martial art, *ki* alignment is the process of aligning your energy flow with your opponent so that you can use his ki to execute a physical action or movement of your choosing, ideally in the direction and angle of your choice. You may supplement his ki with yours or use his ki only if the alignment is proper and complete.

ki flow
Ki flow is the direction that you and your attacker's ki travels and is sometimes referred to as momentum.

kinesthetics
Kinesthetics is the study of the relationship between the skeletal structure and movement.

kubi shimi waza*
Kubi = neck; *shimi* = pain, choke or strangling; *waza* = technique.

kuzushi
Kuzushi is the ability to maintain your balance. It also means maintaining your balance while unbalancing your opponent physically and/or mentally.

leverage
Leverage is a mechanical advantage (ability) achieved by using a lever to move an object.

levers (three kinds)
In physics (and the martial arts), there are three kinds of levers:

1) In a first-class lever, the fulcrum (F) is in between the effort (E) and load (L). First-class levers are frequently used for judo throws and joint locks.

2) In a second-class lever, the load (L) lies in between the effort (E) and the fulcrum (F). The second-class lever is used for some winding and "drop" types of judo throws as well as some choking techniques.

3) In a third-class lever, the effort (E) lies in between the load (L) and the fulcrum (F). This type of lever is usually used to deliver hits and kicks.

ligament
A ligament is a fibrous tissue that connects bones together.

lock (as in locked joint)
A lock is the point at which a joint is bent at 90 degrees so that the lower extremity is facing the upper extremity and is in line with the z-axis of the joint. The lower joint is then rotated (or torqued) along the length

(y-axis) of the extremity to the point at which joint dampening occurs, thus causing the process to continually repeat itself up the y-axis of the extremity until the parent joint is affected.

mae maki senaka shimi waza*
Forward shoulder-roll lock. *Mae* = forward; *maki* = wind; *senaka* = back (shoulder); *shimi* = pain, choke or strangling; *waza* = technique.

maitte
Maitte means "I submit!" It is used to indicate submission in either martial arts training or competition. If the person being submitted cannot say "maitte," he may also tap his opponent or use any extremity (hand, foot, head) to "tap out" on the mat.

MMA
MMA are the initials for mixed martial arts, a relatively recent phenomenon.

momentum
Momentum is the speed you are moving a mass in a particular direction. See **p** = mv.

mushin
Mushin is a state of mind (or non-mind) in which the individual is so competent at a particular task (or series of related tasks) that no conscious effort is being expended to accomplish the task(s). A person in this state of mind will have little or no recollection of what actually happened but thinks that whatever he did was done in a competent manner and with success.

off-balancing
Off-balancing is the process of moving a person out of vertical alignment with his y-axis, usually at his center point which is normally perpendicular to the ground. (See *hara*, *saiki tanden*, zero point or humanoid joint)

origin point (of x, y, z)
In a three-dimensional graph, this is the zero point where the x, y, and z axes intersect with each other.

p = mv (explain elements of formula)

This is the basic (simple) formula for determining the momentum of an object. In this formula, "p" (bold "**p**") = momentum, m = mass (amount of matter being moved) and v = velocity (the speed at which the mass is moving).

pain

Pain is the intensity of an electrical signal from a nerve to your brain, indicating the amount of discomfort, injury or harm to a particular part of your body. Pain does not necessarily or always indicate serious injury to the body. Pain and injury are two entirely different things, although the latter (injury) will cause the former (pain) to occur. Sudden, high levels of pain can cause the brain to become unconscious, even momentarily, if the shock to the human system is too great. At lower levels, pain inducement through nerve and pressure points can cause your opponent to lose motor control of the affected extremity and even his entire body if the pressure applied and technique used is effective.

pain compliance

Pain compliance is the process of using particular holds, locks and/or pressure (nerve) points to secure the physical cooperation of your opponent. Most *jujitsu* black belts and advanced students in jujitsu are highly skilled at using pain-compliance techniques because it usually is an integral part of their training. A talented jujitsu practitioner can sense his opponent's level of discomfort through his body language and movement, which allows the practitioner to use the minimum amount of discomfort necessary to make his opponent comply.

pronation

Pronation occurs when you turn an extremity inward toward the body along the extremity's y-axis.

sacrum

The sacrum comprises five connected vertebrae that form joints with the hipbones and stabilize the pelvis.

saiki tanden

The *saiki tanden* is the center point of the human body, about two inches below the navel. See also *hara*, zero point or center point.

senaka shimi waza*
Shoulder-lock pin. *Senaka* = back (shoulder); *shimi* = pain, choke or strangling; *waza* = technique.

set (technique is "set")
A hold is set when all the necessary joints are locked and your *ki* is relaxed and in alignment with your opponent to the extent that any resistance on his part will result in discomfort, pain, injury, and/or the follow-through execution of the technique through the opponent's efforts rather than your own (the defender).

submission
A submission is when sufficient additional pressure, leverage, joint dampening or other action is applied to a hold or lock to cause your opponent to submit (*maitte* or tap out) or risk injury to the affected joint as a result of his noncompliance. Most submissions are figure-4 locks.

supination
Supination occurs when you turn an extremity outward away from the body along the extremity's y-axis.

takedown
A takedown is when the attacker is placed in a lock or hold and brought down to the ground in a controlled manner by the defender. Most involve the use of figure-4 locks. One or both of the attacker's feet remain on the ground throughout execution of the takedown. A takedown may be finished off with a submission.

tatami
Tatami are the rice mats originally used by martial artists to land on when they were thrown in a traditional *dojo*. Tatami have been replaced by various types of foam mats that may be placed on various types of floors, some of which have great shock-absorption capabilities on their own.

te no shioku nage*
Nerve attack hand throw. *Te* = hand, *no* = a grammatical transitional possessive phrase, *shioku* = nerve, *nage* = throw.

tendon
A tendon is a band of fibrous tissue that connects muscle and bone together.

tendon/ligament limitations
This is the limit that tendons and ligaments can be pulled or twisted without being damaged or torn. Most conscientious martial artists try to avoid reaching such limitations in practice because of the serious nature of such injuries, the extremely long length of time required for proper healing and the ease of re-injury.

throw
A throw occurs when the defender uses the attacker's *ki* momentum, energy, leverage, locks or holds in any combination to cause the attacker to have both feet in the air as the technique is executed. A throw can be finished off with a submission, if necessary.

torque
Torque is the amount of effort, energy or force applied to the twisting motion around an axis, usually the y-axis. Excessive torquing can result in joint injury and torque or "green branch" fractures.

traditional jujitsu
Traditional *jujitsu* is a term given to older systems of jujitsu in which most of the techniques, holds and submissions are done from a standing position or by momentarily dropping down onto one knee when necessary. Although most techniques can also be executed from a formal sitting position (*sutemi waza*), from a chair or even lying down, traditional jujitsu practitioners will avoid going to the ground unless they are in a safe position to do so.

ude gatame*
Shoulder-lock pin. *Ude* = arm, *gatame* = grapple.

ude guruma*
Armbar. *Ude* = arm, *guruma* (*kuruma*) = circular (wraparound).

ude guruma*
Arm lock. *Ude* =arm, *guruma* (*kuruma*) = circular (wraparound).

ude guruma*

Proper arm lock. *Ude* = arm, *guruma* (*kuruma*) = circular (wrap-around).

ude guruma*

Standing rear arm lock. *Ude* = arm, *guruma* (*kuruma*) = circular (wrap-around).

ude maki shimi waza*

Shoulder-lock wind press. *Ude* = arm; *maki* = wind; *shimi* = pain, choking or strangling; *waza* = technique.

ude makikomi*

Arm wind. *Ude* = arm, *makikomi* = wind.

ude makikomi shimi waza*

Elbow-lock wrist press. *Ude* = arm; *makikomi* = winding throw; *shimi* = pain, choking or strangling; *waza* = technique.

ude no shimi waza*

Shoulder lock. *Ude*=arm; *no*= a grammatical transitional possessive phrase; *shimi*=pain, choke or strangling; *waza*=technique.

ude senaka shimi waza*

Shoulder lock. *Ude* = arm; *senaka* = back (shoulder); *shimi* = pain or strangling; *waza* = technique.

zero point

See *hara*, *saiki tanden*, center point.

Notes

Italics
All words in italics are phonetic transliterations of Japanese terminology. Different sources may present different spellings in an attempt to get the same "sounds."

*(asterisk)
An asterisk appears when the name of a technique appears in this glossary. Jack Sanzo Seki (my *sensei*) used a lot of generic terminology to name the techniques he taught, so the Japanese and English titles may not match exactly. Different styles of *jujitsu* use different names for the same techniques (in English and Japanese), depending on who was the first person to write the name of the technique down. This problem exists in other martial arts, as well. The same problem also exists in other languages that try for transliterations.

Sometimes the terminology Seki used referred to the defender's actions while executing a particular *kata*. Sometimes the terminology referred to what happened to the attacker. Lastly (and most frustrating), Seki would use different terms for the same techniques; if you watched his execution carefully, you could usually pick up slight variations that justified the variations in the Japanese terminology.

Surprisingly, most *jujitsuka*, regardless of style or country of origin, prefer to use the Japanese terminology because it makes effective technical communication simpler.

BLACK BELT®
World's Leading Magazine of Martial Arts

HOME   STYLES   VIDEOS   ARCHIVES   INTERACTIVE   MARKETPLACE   SHOP   DOJO DIRECTORY

HALL OF FAME
Search *Black Belt's* online cache of articles for
a wide variety of topics, names, styles and
more!

Search

Register Now

Find your martial arts style   GO

ARCHIVE FEATURE

George Kirby:
2007 Instructor of the Year

✉ EMAIL   🖨 PRINT

George Kirby:
2007 Instructor of the Year

By Jon Sattler

For some, teaching is nothing more than a steady
paycheck. For *jujutsu* master George Kirby, it's a
calling that he's uniquely and undeniably suited for.

Long before the Brazilian *jiu-jitsu* revolution swept the
United States, the amiable Kirby began studying the
gentle art to help deal with the stress of grad school.
Little did he know that his tutelage under sensei Jack
"Sanzo" Seki was the beginning of a martial arts
journey that would shape America's understanding of
jujutsu for decades to come.

By 1968, Seki could sense Kirby's potential as an
instructor and told him and fellow-student Bill Fromm
about an opening at a local YMCA in Burbank, California.
When Kirby pointed out that as brown belts they were
too inexperienced to teach, Seki responded, "Now
you're both black belts. Act like it."

And so began the teaching career of one of traditional
jujutsu's most respected and beloved masters. A year
later, Kirby followed another one of Seki's suggestions
and collaborated with Fromm to form the American
Ju-Jitsu Association. Under Kirby's stewardship, first

George Kirby
(Photo by Thomas Sanders)

as president and now as chairman, the AJA has grown into a governing body renowned for bringing together
jujutsu practitioners from around the world. He's also the founder and chairman of the Budoshin Ju-Jitsu Dojo
Inc., a nonprofit educational foundation, and the Budoshin Ju-Jitsu Yudanshakai, a research and educational
foundation.

Kirby's collaborations are too numerous to list in their entirety, but a few of the groups he's donated his time to
helping are the Budo Centre International, Nippon Seibukan, Shorinji Ryu Jujitsu Association and World Head of
Family Sokeship Council.

Despite his busy schedule as an ambassador of the arts, teaching has always been Kirby's passion. Following his
sensei's advice, Kirby taught jujutsu and self-defense at the Burbank YMCA until 1974, when he received an
opportunity to expand his program with the Burbank Parks and Recreation Department. His partnership with the
city lasted until 1996, when he decided to take on the challenge of launching a new jujutsu program for the city
of Santa Clarita, California, where he continues to share what he's learned. Along the way, he perfected his craft
in the public-school system, where he taught jujutsu and social studies for nearly four decades.

Following the Rodney King controversy, Kirby worked with a handful of other nationally known martial artists to
develop for the Los Angeles Police Department what would become one of the nation's best arrest-and-control
training programs. In 1998 the city of Los Angeles awarded him a Certificate of Appreciation for his role as a
defensive-tactics consultant on the Civilian Martial Arts Advisory Panel.
The LAPD isn't the only organization to recognize Kirby's outstanding work. The California Branch Jujitsu
Federation twice awarded him the title of Outstanding Instructor, and he's earned the Amateur Athletic Union
Jujitsu National Sports Award and a certificate of honor from the Federation of Practicing Jujutsuans.

His dedication to teaching extends well beyond the classroom and the dojo. A prolific writer, Kirby has penned a
half-dozen books on jujutsu, and his essays have appeared in numerous publications, including *Black Belt*. He's
also preserved his teachings digitally with an eight-part DVD study course.

In 2000 Kirby reached the pinnacle of his profession when he was promoted to *judan*, or 10-degree black belt.
In recognition of his 40 years of teaching, *Black Belt* is proud to induct him into its Hall of Fame as 2007

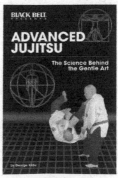